Selected Poems from

Through The Eyes of Enid

Enid Pickett

EP

ENID PICKETT PRESS
California

Paperback ISBN: 979-8-218-47387-7

First printing edition 2024

enidpickett.com

4

To Our Children

"We must support our children in every way we can. We must allow our children freedom to express themselves creatively. We must praise our children and thank them for their gift of inspiration. We must motivate our children spiritually. We must challenge our children to a higher level of achievement. We must increase our children's self-confidence and improve their overall quality of life." We must love our children.

"So, we say to our children, draw, paint, write, act, sing, dance, build, think, explore, question, express, play, and be free to dream always."

Words inspired by Tupac Shakur

Children are the reward of life. — Zaire proverb

Thank You Tomorrows for Being.
Keep Sankofa in your pockets.
Aaliyah Sims
Amalio Aguilar
Anella Narcisi Hume
Athena J. Abdullah
Bilal K. Abdullah
Brian Jr. Reid
Captain Jordan Marcus
Chase Reed
Coy Reed

Fatima J. Abdullah
Giavanna Humphreys
Ifetayo Newman-Grimsley
Jaafar T. Abdullah
James Love
Jasmine Hopkins
Joey Holliday
Josiah Reid
Jules Von Terflinger
Macai Collier
Madisyn Sims
Mason Collier
Mikai Reid
Mila Rowe Garcia
Muhammad J. Abdullah
Nah' Sahn Sims
Natalia Humphreys
Nehemiah Farmer
Nehemiah Reid
Ny' Arah-Areatha Sims
Noah Orion Burnley & Dillon Randall
Prince Sims
Riley Sims
Rylan Bowers
Sanai Sims
Sophia Humphreys
Whitney Gray Hopkins
Zephaniah Reid
Zeus Love

Contents

Avowals & Acknowledgments

This book is your Garden of Gratitude. Each person is a flower flourishing with
Succulent Sacred Seeds. Thank You for Being…
Enid Pickett
Painters use Colors. Poets use Words.

Thank you to My Ancestors…
Alice Doggett, Ethel Williams, Thomas H. Williams, Dorothy Walker, Ernestine Jones, Areatha Sims, Buster Pickett, Jean Elise Pickett, Alice Lawson, Bill Lawson, Uncle "Buck" William Doggett, Aunt Edna Doggett, Delly Woolridge, Bobby Woolridge, Rose Woolridge, Donnelly Woolridge, Robyn Woolridge.

Thank you to the Ancestors in Training. Thank You for Being…
Thank you, *Sierra Dylan Pickett*, my Baller, Magnificent, Cherished, Lovechild, Daughter.
I love you madly.
Thank you for Being…Gerald & Helene Pickett, Freddie Pickett, Joey Pickett, Queenie Pickett, Larry Lawson, Valeria Lawson, Loryn Lawson, Ray Reed, Beverly Sims, Andre' X. Sims, Nicole Ligon, Gerald A. Sims, Heide Arroyo, Donyae Sims, Celena L. Sims, Kim Collier, Sean Collier, Barbara Greenwood-Scott, Mateen Kemet, Erinn Anova, Sela Kerr.

Forever Forest Flowers
Bloom during Full Moonlight.
Listen. Tiny blossoms smile as
They serenade their seeds secretly.

Thank you for Being... Andy Jones, Anissa Burnley Humphreys, Brian Reid, Brian Simmons, Carlton Page, Chinouyazura Dotson-Newman, Christopher Bowers, Dylan Atler, Graham Humphreys, Healdsburg Freedom Jazz Choir, Jaim L. Foster, James Randall Harrison, Joe Garcia, Josh Klor & Melanie, Mani Simmons, Melecio Estrella, N'Game Gray, Noah Hume, Nzinga Dotson-Newman, Ogonnaya Dotson-Newman, ReEllis Dotson-Newman, Phil Vieux, Bill Newman, Sabryyah & Ali Abdullah, Samuel Fleming Lewis.

Pillars & Milestones
I have had rare opportunities to
Know and Love extraordinary human beings.
Thank you all for being my muse... Abiodun Oyewole, Aduku Utah, Alixa Garcia, Caitlin Elizabeth, Destiny Muhammed, John Santos, Marc Bamuthi Joseph, Marcus Shelby, Naima Penniman, Peggy McIntosh, Tiffany Austin

Did you know...

Enid Pickett has been writing poetry since she was a child. She won a poetry contest while attending Findlay University, Findlay, Ohio. She won first prize; tickets to see Jimi Hendrix.

This embarked her poetic journey studying poets such as June Jordan, Maya Angelou, The Last Poets, Nikki Giovanni, bell hooks, and Tupac Shakur.

Her influences include the wisdom of, Toni Morrison, Isabel Wilkerson, Tim Wise, Angela Davis, Cornel West, Sweet Honey and the Rock, Nina Simone, Miles Davis, Bruce Springsteen, Gregory Porter, Abbey Lincoln, Joni Mitchell, Wes Montgomery, Carlos Santana and John Coltrane.

Her poetry paths crossed in Healdsburg, California. Meeting Jessica Felix, Founder of the Healdsburg Jazz Festival and Marcus Shelby, Artistic Director of Healdsburg Jazz, along with Tiffany Austin, Choir Director of the Healdsburg Freedom Jazz Choir. She sang in the Healdsburg Freedom Jazz Choir for over ten years.

Recognizing her talent, Shelby invited her to be the first Artist in Residence as their Poet Laureate in 2020. She and the Marcus Shelby Jazz Band performed at the historic San Francisco Jazz Center honoring Duke Ellington. In 2023, they performed at SF Jazz Center for the United Nations 75th Celebration of Human Rights. They have performed at several events with Healdsburg Jazz and around northern California.

Enid has collaborated and performed with Destiny Muhammad, John Santos, Faye Carol, Kenny Washington, Lewis Watts, Carlton Page AKA, Writ3rtha 3rd, Kennan Webster, Stella Heath, Sylvia Cuenca, Tammy Lynne Hall, and many more musicians and other artists.

Did you know Enid performs regularly with Abiodun Oyewole of the Last Poets in an amazing Open House forum with poets from all over the world?

Poets who have inspired Enid are very close to her heart. Marc Bamuthi Joseph, Climbing Poetree, Naima Penniman, Alixa Garcia, Aduka Utah, Saul Williams, and the San Francisco Youth Speaks Slam Poets.

Foreword

As unique and impactful as Enid Pickett is, mom is also mom. She's my "normal." It's easy to forget that everyone has a different take on what is routine and commonplace in our everyday lives. This book in your hands is not only a reminder to me personally of how special my mom is, it also is an opportunity to examine hard work, passionate dedication, grit, and perseverance, all those behind-the-scenes ingredients that make a dream come true. It is my extreme honor to accompany her pages with some of my own ink, introducing you to her.

You may have come across Enid Pickett in her classrooms. Decades of education hidden in-between school chalkboards and vinyl floors, ringing bells, colored pencils and workbooks stacked on each desk. Her library is drool-worthy. Mom is and always will be an educator. She has guided hundreds (dare I say more) students, generations of students, as a Grand-Master teacher. A family tree passing on leaf to branch to root, Ms. Pickett's students have a lineage of each generation seeking out her welcoming classroom's wisdom and kindness. Mom gets down on one knee to make the students feel seen and known, while spending countless hours striving for their best with all her might.

Maybe you met Enid in one of her workshops exploring Ethnic Integrity and courageous conversations, dismantling the dynamics of oppression through macro and micro lenses. She's facilitated workshops globally with new parents in transracial adoptions and larger audiences including the California State Teachers state union members and officials, the National Education Association, designing Summer Institutes at Sonoma State University with the North Bay International Studies Project, the Fulbright Foundation, National SEED (Seeking Educational Equity and Diversity) Project, and NAME (National Association for Multicultural Education). I've cut my teeth on concepts of intersectionality and social justice at the dinner table and passing out handouts at her workshops, when I first started walking. These ideas and values run through her and are reflected in all she does.

Maybe you know mom from her skills in the kitchen. Mama, Grandma Dot, and Aunt Areatha taught Enid to put her foot in it and she does, often. Gumbo, cornbread, brownies, fancy meals and simple snacks, Mom is the utmost nourisher. One who can mix sweet and savory in all forms. She utilizes presentation and adds an artistic flair to stylize the plating and even indulges in cooking shows to elevate her craft.

Or you could have seen her at a concert, a true jazz aficionado. Mom's music is unscripted, alive and layered finding many meanings. A singer and spoken-word artist herself, she's an enthusiast of all instruments, performing for a decade with the Healdsburg Freedom Jazz Choir, several Juneteenth festivals, and even at SF Jazz. Enid can connect the musical notes and words by the sound of her voice.

To add even more dimensions, I can talk about her humor, kindness, dance moves, intelligence, Virgo skills, how she's a film enthusiast, and her vigilant loyalty buoyed with an unapologetic goofiness. Ultimately, I'm here to showcase Enid Pickett's pen, before she shows you its core.

One of my earliest memories of existence is listening to my mom's voice. She would hum and sing our secret song, read, recite, and story-tell constantly, even before my ears were independent of the womb. She created her own imaginative series of bedtime stories that introduced me to poetry and a playful side of language before I even knew what it was, beginning all the words with the same letter. *An absolutely auspicious and adventurous activity enjoyed each evening*! Since those tucked-under-the-covers nights all those years ago, alliteration continues to be one of our favorite expressions of wordsmithing, and she endeavors to breathe life into it frequently.

Albeit new(ish) to me, mom has always written, in college and her own secret manuscripts. I have witnessed a full channeling, as the spirit of a poem comes through her and she must pour it on paper, its "bones," almost a divining. Holding the sacred in these words both her and the known/unknown, inviting you to listen and feel, and pay your most profound gift forward - *pay attention*. These moments of words on a page act as a portal, bringing time and memories, hope and future-dreams into what is real, right now. She spins you in circles and washes you in rhyme or prose. She connects your senses to heart and to mind, as you're unsure which is the start or end.

Enid Pickett is a poet.
These are her words.

Sierra Dylan Pickett

Preface

Life sometimes delivers moments that feel as powerful as a cosmic explosion. Hearing Enid Pickett read her poetry for the first time was like seeing a shooting star light up the night.

I first saw Enid read her poem, *Juneteenth Ancestors are African*, at a Freedom Festival event, celebrating independence from Juneteenth to Independence Day. Her voice was a powerful, loving force, radiating through the room. I was one of many, springing to my feet to give her a much-deserved standing ovation.

For days afterward, I carried her words with me. Since then, I've had the pleasure and honor of helping Enid compile her decades of work into this book. And I've been lucky enough to hear the stories behind these poems: of the people she loves, the places she's been, and the wisdom she carries.

Enid is a supernova. A luminous explosion of bright light, birthing new ideas for a new way to live. Her poetic words are here to illuminate hearts and minds.

I was offered a gift the day I sat in a crowd and heard her poetry. Now, you get to experience her gifts too. And see the world, through her eyes.

With forever gratitude,
caitlin elizabeth

Through The Eyes of Enid

Alliteration Alphabet Poem

A children's nonsense poem.

Always Abnormal
Big. Beautiful.
Colorfully Courageous.
Delightfully Dramatic.
Equally Exciting
Fantastic Fairytales Foods!

Gigantic Green Giggling Grapes
Heavy. Hollow. Hidden.
Inside Identical
Jumping Jelly-Jam Jars.

Knighted Kismet Kings
Lightheartedly Listen
Making Magical Moon Muffins,
Notorious Nutcracker Noodles,
Purple Pickle Pokemon Popcorn,
Questionable Quality Quail Quivers

Remember Royal
Ruffian Raisins?
Small, Sticky,
Sour and Sweet?
Tasty, Tongue Tickling
Ugly and Unafraid
Very Victorious.
Wiggling.Waggling.

Wailing.
While Wilting,
Willting,
Wilting.
Xmas and Xboxes
Yelling.
Yes, Yelling.
"Zap"
Zigzag"
And Zippy"

Anatomy of a Soul

A Calm, Cool Peaceful Presence.
A Nameless, Faceless Being.
An Ageless, Adoring, Ancestral Essence.
An Infinite, Intimate Silence.

SomeWhere. SomePlace. SomeTime.
Between Ecstasy and the Exosphere.
Between Now and Next.
Between Beginning and Ending.

Five Free Falling Stars
Whisper their Forgotten Names.

Their Shattered, Shaded
Slivered Shadows Shine and Shine.
Singing Silent Harmonies.
As they Shape Shift with
Iced X-Rayed Inner Visions.

Imprinting
Wishing Well Wishes.
Mama's melted Memories.
Daddy's Dreams and Seeds.
Premature Happiness.
Pregnant Possibilities
All
God Gifted by Grace.
Wrapped in Withered Wrinkled

Egyptian Papyrus.
Waiting. Wondering.
Waiting. Wondering.
Waiting for The
Newborn
To Open.

A Poem Called Freedom

Freedom Sleeps
With one eye open.
Her best friend is named Hope.
She writes Poetry
Every Friday night
With the Last Poets.
She Walks in
Shoes that Whisper.
Everybody knows her Name.
FREEDOM. FREEEEEDOM
FreedomFriends includes...
Unconventional, Radical, Nonconforming,
Revolutionary
Warriors
Change-Agents
Activists
Artists
Educators
And so many more.
Join Freedom
Downtown at her place.
Between Liberation Boulevard
and
Independence Avenue
For A
Sweet Meet and Greet.
Casually Converse
with your

Unsung, Unbought, Unbossed,
Brothers and Sisters.
They all Know Freedom.
They Know her Intimately.
They love her.
They adore her.
They kill for her.
They will protect,
Honor and defend her.

You can find Freedom
Deep down inside
John Coltrane's mouth.
She wildly waits
As she Wraps around
Miles' fingers.
Freedom
Sings and Sings and Sings
With Ella's voice.
Freedom jumps off
A cliff
Looks Up!
And Always
Land on her feet.
Freedom is Fearlessly Ensconced
in
Everything Ebony.
Onyx Ocean Waves Echo
Echo Echo
Her Harmonious Heartbeats.

Her Grandmother's name is
MaMaWisdom.
Freedom loves to
Daily DayDream
With her cousins…
Liberty
Autonomy
And Justice.
Freedom sleeps with anyone she wants to.
Her clothes are invisible.
Her hair is carefully colored camouflage.
When She yells status quo quakes.
Her favorite food is Everything.
She is never late.
She is never Alone.
Her Dreams tell the Future.

Freedom sleeps
With one eye open.
Her best friend is named Hope.
She writes Poetry
Every Friday night
With the Last Poets.

Her Face can shift shape in a second.
Harriet, Biko, Duke
Tony Morrison
Tupac, Angela, Maya,
James Baldwin
HipHop, and Kehinde Wiley.

Freedom Travels
24/7/3 6 5.
She needs no passport.
No money. No invitation.
No Borders.
Freedom's Favorite Cousins
Always Cookin up
Something.
Siblings: Economic and Artistic,
Twin Cousins: Science and Academic.
Her oldest cousin is always close by.
They call her Political.
Freedom Fights for
All
Oppressed.
All Imprisoned.
All In Unjust
Prison Zones.
Physical and Mental
Prison Zones, too.
Freedom Babies
Each born premature
With untold stories
Carved into history.
Some were born. Decades old.
Freedom named her Maiden Babies
Speech.
Wonder.
Live.
Think.

Open.
Safe.
Love.

Freedom will live forever.
She will always be there.
Whispering in your ear.
And
she
sleeps
with one eye open.
Her best friend is named Hope.
And
She writes Poetry
Every Friday night
With the Last Poets.

A Poem for Ava

Ava
Absolute Appreciation
Appointed Aquatic Apogee
Everyone Agrees
Swimmers in the Deep End
Swimmers in the Spa
Swimmers in the Shallow End
And
All the Life Guards
Admire Affectionately
and
Appreciate
Ava
The Friendliest Mermaid in Windsor
She Swims with Admiration
She Swims with Appreciation
She Swims with Sincere Self-Assurance
She Swims and Smiles
She Swims and Smiles
So Agile Everyday
She Swims With a Friendly Hello
She is our Gift
Always Greeting
Always Guiding
Us To enjoy another day at the pool
another day
with
Ava's Accolades of Appreciation and Joy.

Before

Before.
We've All been here Before.
We've smelled that Familiar Scent of
Urgency.
That Pathological Passion Fruit.
That immediate Fearlessness of
Blood Stained Convictions
Confused with Crumbs of
Casual Courage.

Before.
Before Mother Nature
Father Time
Share their intricate
Intimate instruments.

Before.
We really Over Come.
Before
We Lift every Voice and sing...
Remember. Remember.

We have All
Seen This
All Before.

As long as we remember to...feel.
As long as we remember to...fight.

As long as we remember to...cry.
As long as we remember to...love.

You will always be there, Harriet.

Humming.
Humming.
Humming in our ears.

Be Free.
Be Free.
Be Free.

Be Glorious.
Be Glorious.
Be Glorious.

Harriet Tubman
You are NOT GONE.
No...No...No.
Your Spirit will never die.
You will NOT REST
In Peace.

Your Sacred Scars
Disguised as
Destiny in
Dirt Colored Skin.
They know the "Way"
Look Close.
Touch in-between

Those Scars.
Let your fingers
Find Those Painful Paths.
Look deep, deep down
Follow the Mystery.
Follow the Misery Map.
Your Fingers will find their Way.

They Know. They Know.

They tell your story.
They know your name.

We know your name.
Harriet Tubman.
Your words are seeds
To be planted
For generations
To come.

You said,
"Every Great Dream
Begins with a dreamer.
Always remember
You have within you
The Strength.
The Patience.
And the Passion
To reach for the stars."

Your Weathered wisdom is
More powerful
Harriet Beyond this veil.

Thank You. Thank You.
Thank You.
For Being One
Of the **Real Ones.**
Today.
Yesterday.
Tomorrow.

Black n Blues

Sweet
Smiling Satchmo
Soul Bearing Rhapsodies, Spirituals, Show tunes
And lots, and lots of songs.

Songs.
Some songs too sad
To be called a song.

Songs.
Served with fresh slices of *"Strange Fruit*
Hanging from the Popular tree."

Songs.
That make you tap your toes
Even while you are dreaming.

Songs.
That silently slipped over the Color line
While doing the Cake Walk.

Songs.
Hit you so deep, in places and spaces
You almost forgot.

Songs.
Dressed like spies that whisper lost and stolen memories.

Songs.
Flavored with the scent of blood stained indigo.

Songs.
Smell like hot beignets baked for your auditory palette,
all savory, saucy, and sweet, so bittersweet,
it soothes your soul.

1929
Dr. Martin Luther King, Jr was born.
Black and Blue Blues
Gave birth to twins that same year.
Humming and slumming as some
Soundtrack for the stories
History will never tell.

1955
The year Rosa Parks refused to give up her seat on the front of
the bus,
in Montgomery, Alabama.
Sweet Smiling Satchmo contributed to the Civil Rights
movement with...
"My only sin is in my skin
What did I do to be so black and blue?"

1955
Brown v Board of Education.
A pivotal win.
The Supreme Court ruled, all classrooms will be integrated in
the United States of America.

You could hear Sweet Smiling Satchmo sing...
"I'm white inside but that don't help my case
Cause I can't hide my face."

1955
Emmett Till
One of countless others
Murdered or worse.
He knew. He heard.
Sweet Smiling Satchmo slowly sing...

"Cold empty bed springs
Hard as lead."

Not as hard as the lead in Flint families' water.

Sweet Smiling Satchmo sang...
"Cold empty bed springs
Hard as lead.
Feels like O'l Ned
Wished I was dead."

2016
Today is yesterday.
We still hear Sweet Smiling Satchmo.
Parallel lines never cross.

Today is yesterday.
Over a half century of yesterdays
Black and Brown voices sing the blues

On streets named Oppression and
Dr.Martin Luther King, Jr. Way.

Today and yesterday worsened by
Masking what History did to be so black and blue.

Some say fear controls the answers.
Some say only Truth and Hope will be
The answer beyond the paradigm and crime
We were all born into.

"How will it end, ain't got a friend.
What did I do be so black and blue?"

Black History

Black History
Black His-Story
We are surrounded
In our daily lives by Black History.
Today, we celebrate
The Scientists, The Mathematicians, The Engineers,
The Inventors, The Creative Artists & The Brilliant Thinkers.
That encircles us. Embrace us.
Comfort, Care & Carry us 24/7 365.

Did you know???
Black History changed our world?
With innovation, Imagination, Inspiration & Information.
Let's celebrate & honor those Black Brave Brilliant
Masterminds that gave us
Their inventions we have in our homes, our lives, & our
world.
Here's a few examples to enlighten your mind.
The lock to keep us free from danger.
The eggbeater. The Air Conditioner.
The disposable syringe to keep us alive.
Home security system to keep us safe.

The lawn mower for manicured grass.
Laser fuels much stronger than gas.
The pencil sharpener we use daily in class.
The elevator, much better than the stairs.
The Gas Mask, the hairbrush to untangle our hair.

Let us not forget the Folding Chair.
We have the heating furnace to keep away the cold.
The cell phone, guitar & the mop
To keep our floors like gold.

The helicopter, Blood Plasma, The Roller Coaster.
We all have Refrigerators and Clothes Dryers too.

Now, look at the Black History
On the bottom of your feet.
A Black Inventor created the shoe, isn't that a treat?
Hold on, there's much more.
What would we do
Without the Traffic Signal?
The Fire Escape Ladder?
Auto Air Brakes?
The Pacemaker Controls?
The Fire Extinguisher too?

Did you know Black History invented
Some of our favorite foods?
Raise your hand if you love ice cream.
I know I do.
We all love Ice Cream. Potato chips. & Peanut Butter.
We drink Black History Coffee every day.
We eat Jambalaya & Red Beans and Rice
Oh, so nice.
There's so many more foods we could taste.
Let's continue to drop dimes about Black History in this place.
So, the next time

You think of one these inventions,
Think and Thank those who made a difference in our lives.
Think of Where & When
Many of those Black Inventors lived.
During Dangerous Jim Crow & Segregated Times
Not that long ago.
They persevered,
They struggled.
&
They succeeded you see.
Black Intelligentsia benefits both you and me.
They succeeded to show & teach the world

That slaves never came from Africa.
Slaves did not come from Africa.
Scientists. Architects. Poets. Mathematicians.
Artists. Engineers. Philosophers. Farmers.
Teachers. Healers. Builders. Inventors
came from Africa.

Thank you, Black History Inventors.
We will never forget you.

You made a difference in our world,
& our everyday lives.

Remember Black History is Every day.

Broken Promises

Have you Forgotten? Have you Forgiven?
All those who Broke a Promise to You?
Promises like…
To Love, Honor, In Sickness. In Health.
To Agree to Disagree. To Remember to follow-through
When they said.
Have you Forgotten? Have you Forgiven?
Yourself?
For breaking a promise
To someone special? To someone important?
To Yourself?

Let's imagine a promise 402 years old.
Now. You understand
What type of promise
This poem is about.
The Promise. To Be Free.
A Promise You Thought You'd Never
Touch. Feel. See.
The Promise to Be Free. To be Real.
That's the Broken Promise of Chattel Slavery.
The Promise to Change… History.
The Promise to Change…
The Heart of a Human Being.
The Promise with
The Greatest Gift of Life

Buried deep inside this Promise.
Freedom. Freedom.

The United States of America.
Land of the Free & Home of the Slave.
What is A Broken Promise?
Empty words = Empty Deeds.
Enslaved African Ancestors
Know well the Stings and Blisters
Of Broken Promises.

1865. U.S. Union Army Officer General Gordon Granger
Carried this Promise.
To Galveston, Texas.
He delivered the news
Two Years in the Shade.
To a small island hanging off the Gulf Coast.
Felix Haywood heard it. He said,
"The end of the war come jus' like that-like you snap your fingers…
Hallelujah broke out.
Soldiers, all of a sudden, was everywhere
Coming in bunches. Everyone was a singin'.
We was all walking' on golden clouds.
Everybody went wild…We was free.
Just like that
We was free."
Or…Was he?
Was he given The Broken Promise of Freedom?

This year. This June. This day.

What Will You Be Given?
Another Broken Promise of Freedom?

Give Glory & Gratitude
To those Taken.
Honor those
Who were There.

Remember…

Our Effortlessly Murdered.
Our Tragically Tortured.
Over this Broken Promise.

Remember…

Hidden Histories. Mama Memories.
Stolen. Erased.
Honor them with Sacred Silence and Prayers.

For…
We are the Holders of Truth and Memory.
We are the Seeds of Daydreams.
We are the Ones.
Shout. Sing out their Names.
We Know the Secrets. We know the Lies.
We Know the Silent Mysteries.
We Go way Beyond the Veil.
We Slide in between the Shadows
Sleeping deep in Coded Truth of DNA.

Shhhh…

NO MORE BROKEN PROMISES…
Disguised as Antiquated Agreements
Cloaked in Cartoon Contracts
Didactical Declarations of Delusions
Plastic Propaganda. Minimal Miseducation.
Fake News. AKA.
Broken Promises.

What was broken, you ask?

The Promise of Freedom from Slavery.
The Promise of Freedom from Bondage.
To Be Free.
Stop Killing Us. The Promise of Freedom.
To Be Free.
Stop Stealing Us. The Promise of Freedom.
To Be Free.
Stop Hurting Us.
Stop Hunting Us.
The Promise of Freedom.
No more. No more.

"It's been a long time Comin'
But I know a Change Is Gonna Come"
We Hold These Truths to Be Self-Evident.
To be Inherently Free.
To be Independently Free.
Our Voices are Free.

Diverse. Expressive. Intelligent.
Our Voices are Relevant.

Imagine…155 Past Futures ago.
This Broken Promise was born.
Wrapped in blood-stained hemp pages
Of the Emancipation Proclamation
Ink and blood still wet.
Mother and Father
Sitting on slippery slopes of Slave & Master.
Baptized this Baby "Broken Promise."
Nursed on Bittersweet Nectar of Canards.
Carefully Taught to Forswear 155 Birthdays.

1980. This Neonate Became A semi-state holiday.
"Juneteenth."
Close Your Eyes.
Imagine…401 Years of Freedom.
401 Years of Non-violence. 401 Years of Peace.
Look around. What Do You See?
401 Years of Broken Bloody Promises.
Now. Look Deeper with me.
Look Underneath Each Promise.

You See…
Something More. Something Hidden.
Something Rare. Something Wonderful.
You See…
Black Reality. Black Love. Black Integrity.
Black Grace. Black Truth.

BlackIntelligentsia.
Black Honor.
You See…
Black Children. Black Dreams.
Black Promises.

Our Enslaved African Ancestors
Gave Their Black Promises to Us.
To Remember.
Our Blood. Our Skin. Our Bond.
Our Enslaved African Ancestors
Sacrificed Every Thing for Us.

To Have and Hold Memory.
To Have and Hold Memory.

What are your Memories?

"It's Been a Long Time Comin'
It's Been a Long Time Comin'
But I Know a Change Is Gonna Come."

Buster's Original Southern BBQ

Yesterday's Juke Joints
Are Musical Memories
Magical Moments Gone By.
Those Homemade Dreams
Sweet Seasoned Realities
Live In Our Hearts Forever.

Remember...
Walking & Walking & Walking
For Miles & Miles
On One Dirt Road?
Following Your Nose.
Following Your Ears.
They Know the Way...
Your GPS
To the Best of
"The Best."
The Best Music.
The Best Food.
The Best Place.
To Feel... **Free**.

Today,
We No Longer
Have Juke Joints
Hidden Deep Down
In the Woods.

Today, we Have
A "New" Spot
Nestled in Cozy
Calistoga, California.

Today We Have Buster's Southern BBQ.

Every Sun Day After Noon
On the Garden Patio.

The Place
Where You Can Feel
That Deep Down
Juke Joint Spirit.

Coming Back to...
Be FREE.

Listen.
To Soulful Spicy Sounds Simmer & Soothe Your Soul.

Listen.
And You will feel...
FREE.

Stevie Wonder & Herbie Hancock,
B.B. King & Marvin Gaye,
Aretha & Al Green,
Will All Be There
Along with Their Funky Friends,
Classic R & B,

Soul & Rock & Roll.
They Will Rock
Your Ever Living Soul.

Look Around
See Familiar Faces
Some New Ones Too.

You'll Never Know
Who Will "Jam"
With the Band.
Or Sit Next to You
Under the Shade Umbrellas.
Hearts Humming as You Sip
Icy Cold Lemonade.

Don't Forget
Buster's Famous
BBQ Secret Sauce.

All You Need is...
A Cup of Sweet Sax.
One Cup Spicy Guitar.
A Full Cup Honey Hot Keys.
Add Another Cup Savory Sexy Beats
Two cups Black Bottom Bass.

So Freaking Good!

Tastebuds Dance with
Your feet.

Nobody Does It Better.
Buster's Down Home
Southern BBQ
Sunday After Noon
Three Hours
Of Being Free.

Buster Always Says...
"Look Around & You see America."
His Wise Words Linger
With the Fading Sun.
As the Day Fades to an End.

The Crowd Slowly Sips Away.
That's When You Feel It.
That's When You Really Believe

We All Can
Be Free.

Look Around.
Families Smiling.
Heads Nodding.
Feet Tapping
To Your Favorite Beat.

That's Buster's.
That's Buster's Southern BBQ.

Where You Know
You are Free.

Come Join Us.
Every Sun Day.
You Can BE
FREE.

Colors and Contradictions I

1894
Six women bravely followed their dreams.
They were the early pioneers that started
The Saturday Afternoon Club in Santa Rosa, CA.

They organized, strategized, and mobilized.
From the first gatherings in homes.
To the first official meeting in their very own clubhouse.

A place for wives of bankers & businessmen to meet,
Have tea, talk, advocate for women,
Support community improvement,
Promote civic responsibility and
Most importantly,

Educate themselves.

In their service to their community
they became more egalitarian.
This continues today in *The Saturday Afternoon Club*.

Now let's go down memory lane.

1894
Worldly events & experiences
Creeped & crawled & found their way
Into their homes, their lives, even their clubhouse.
It brought **colors & contradictions**

That began in 1894 and still continues today.

Colors & Contradictions of 1894

Gold
The Gold Rush Dust
Lingered in the mines & air.
Every man wanted to strike gold and be rich.
Gold fever found Asian, Native,
Black, White, & Brown women
In prostitution & Bondage.
While Some White women
created Boarding Houses & Sold home goods
To stay alive.
Colors and Contradictions.

Pink
Pink Table linens & lace adorned dinner tables.
In dining rooms of the newly rich and not yet famous.
Pink Parties with Pink champagne from the Gay Nineties.

Pink
Pink Scars on the backs and fronts of
Black & Brown Women
Kidnapped & brought from the South
Enslaved & indentured by their masters to work
Forever in homes & in the fields.

Pink
Stained blood drops from **Slave Revolts & Rebellions**

Decorated the wounds
of those who fought back
endlessly.
Colors and Contradictions.

Green
Money, Money, Money.
Early fortunes were threatened by rumors of a depression.
In a single year, from 1893 to 1894,
Unemployment estimates **increased** from
3% to nearly **19%**
Of **all** working-class Americans.

Those in the upper class invested in Railroads.
Only to lose soon after when businesses and banks began to
fail.
Colors and Contradictions

Red
Extermination
California's relationship with Native Americans
Was fraught with violence, exploitation,
Dispossession and the attempted total
Destruction of tribal communities.

California's first Governor, Peter Burnett,
"[t]hat a war of extermination will continue to be waged
between the two races until the Indian race becomes
extinct..."

Colors and Contradictions

Adobe Red
Father Serra is a controversial figure in California's
mission history.
He is revered by the Catholic Church
for his dedication to the mission system.

Most of his biographers agree
that Serra admired California's Indians,
defending them against abuse,
by soldiers & civilians.
On the other hand,
Serra is viewed by many as one of the primary architects of
the systematic destruction
of the Golden State's native peoples & cultures.

These critics point out that thousands
of Native Americans died while in the missions,
from disease, malnutrition, unsanitary conditions, and
overwork, while
under the paternalistic care of
Father Serra and other
Franciscan friars.
Colors and Contradictions

Red, White Blue
USA USA
My Country Tis of Thee
Song by Jules Levy
Was popular in 1893.

My country, 'tis of thee,
       sweet land of liberty,
       of thee I sing:
       land where my fathers died,
       land of the pilgrims' pride,
       from every mountainside
       let freedom ring!

This song is sung in every public school.
Along with John Philip Sousa
Marches of the 1890's.
The Washington Post March
is still performed in every
High school in California.
However,
The governmental scales of social justice
Have **never** been equal for **ALL** women.
The ERA is proof of that.
Colors and Contradictions.

Colors and Contradictions
Continue to haunt us today.

What will the women of
The *Saturday Afternoon Club* see
When looking into the mirror of the future?

Who and what will they serve?

What colors will they see?

What contributions & contradictions
Will they find?

Will they stand up for
Freedom, justice, and liberation?

Will they see invisible colors or be colorblind?

Will they Hide in plain sight?

What Colors and Contradictions will they see?

Colors and Contradictions II

Earth colors. shades, hues, tints, tones.
Pigment from her natural ways.
Her mood swings every hour.
Growing darker.
Growing lighter.

She sees from midnight covered skies.
Morning sunlight birthing a new dawn.
A single solitary sunray
Destroys her darkness.
Stars dance like scattered fairies
Awakening another new day.
From the deepest depth of the darkest abyss.
Where no light can penetrate her onyx Underworld.
Deaf & Blind with Ebony.

Black
Color of her essence
oil
Secretly secluded
Hidden in her bottomless bowels.
UnDiscovered Destruction & Disease.
Pollution. Plastic. Population.
Killing her softly.
Killing her softly.
Black.
Colors and Contradictions.

Green

Treetops. Leaves. Meadows of Natural Life.
Earth wearing complex clothing
Designer Couture.
Grass. flowers. Flora and Fauna.
Abundant with Vibrant health.
Spring's new Mint wardobe.
Adores Us Organically.
Adorns Us each Spring with Fresh Fashion.
Mother Nature's wear her Birthday Suit on
April's Fool's Day.
Decorated. Celebrated.
Chlorophyll on Steroids.
Yet.
Killing her softly.
Killing her softly.
Pollution.
Fracking.
War. Starvation.
Countless Criminal Currency
Cancer to her core.
Killing her softly.
Killing her softly.
Green
Colors and Contradictions.

Brown

Melanin.
For the Millions.
For the Mountains.

Sand and Soil.
Soil and Sand.
Canyons Grand.
Eyes caramel & tan.
She hears the mudslides
Melting the hills.
Floods & Tornadoes
Cover her skin.
Carpets of dirt live outside in.
Her people casted in
the color of their skin.
Killing her softly.
Killing her softly.
Brown
Colors and Contradictions.

Blue
Skies & Seas
Earth's Favorite Sandwich.
Celestial atmospheres sealed between
Clear Clean
Constant Clouds.
Caribbean Beautiful blue beaches
Bombarded with Acid Rain
Dieing Seas
Chant
"I Can't Breathe"
"I Can't Breathe"
Melting Ice Caps
Sunburned forever

Killing her softly.
Killing her softly.
Blue
Colors and Contradictions.

Earth Inhales & Exhales
She sighs and cries sorrows of sadness.
Life's Rhythmic survival
Balancing birth
Balancing death.
Singing that
Same old Soulful Soundtrack
Da Blues
Praying & humming & moaning
Winds whispering
Bittersweet melancholy
Hope & Desperation
Endless External Pain.
Torture & Torment.
Loss & Forgotten.
Love.
Da Blues
Killing her softly.
Killing her softly.
Blues.
Colors and Contradictions.

White
Clouds Covered Cotton
StarDust hair.

Crystals of snow
Earth frozen with fear
Her bleached Purity
Solid
Soiled, Sullen, Stained. Salted.
Saturated with Greed.
Hate. Hopelessness. Ignorance.
Cleansed with Covert
Cognitive Dissonance.
Confusion mixed with Creative Chaos.
White.
Color+Less
Absence of Colors.
Uniformed Conformity.
Killing her softly.
Killing her softly.
Killing Earth softly.
Colors and Contradictions.

What colors & contradictions do you see?

Denise Perrier - Queen of Spring Fever

Queen Denise Perrier

Crowned Voice with A Heart.

Queen Denise Perrier

Queen of *Swing Fever.*

Born in Louisiana

Beignets in her Blood.

Grew Up in

West Oakland. California

On 15th & Cypress

With Harlem of the West

Jazz Greats.

And.

Her very own

Jukebox

Bumpin' in her

Living Room.

Billie Holiday & Lil Green

Singing & Swinging

From Sweet Sounds in the mornings.

Strange Fruit.

To Why Don't You Do Right?

Royal &Regal Queen Denise Perrier

Satchmo Saw & Heard

You.

Your Sultry.

Soulful.

Smoky.

Sweet

& Savory Voice

Star Dust

Magically Mixed

With Wild Wanderlust

Gracefully Landed

On Your Head.

Leaving Albany High

Passport In Hand.

Your Footprints

Kissed the Ground

In Over 24 Countries.

Russia.

Rio.

Tokyo.

Mexico.

The World Said,

You'd Be So Nice

To Come Home To.

So.

You made the World

Your Home.

Royal & Regal Queen Denise Perrier

You Sing in the

Language of

Love.

Blues.

Soul.

Jazz.

Whispering with a

Hint of Humor & Irony.

In-Between the

Layers of your Lovely Lyrics.

You Sing in

Cabarets

Standing Room Only

Supper Clubs.

Execute Excellence

in

New Orleans

Monterey

Russian River

And the Healdsburg Jazz Festivals.

You Performed Tributes To

Bessie Smith,

Dinah Washington & Billie Holiday.

Your Musical Ancestors.

Show Time At

Lincoln Center

SF Jazz Center

California Jazz Conservatory

Russian Philharmonic Orchestra.

Your Worldly Footprints

Lovingly Leave

Musical Memories.

Queen Denise Perrier

Crowned Queen with A Voice.

Wears Many Hats...

Dancer.

Actor.

Producer.

Traveler.

Velvet Vocalist Extraordinaire.

You Said your muse,

"It's Straight Out of

Ella, Billie, & Sarah."

We say,

It's Straight Out of

Ella.Billie.Sarah

AND

Denise.

History Knows Your Name.

Denise Perrier.

Thank You.

Merci.

Gracias.

Obrigada,

Ta'Ta.

Thank You.

Early in the Morning

Early Morning Dew Drops
Cleanse the Chilled virgin air.
You can barely hear.
Old Man Father Frosts'
Ritual of Cussin' her out.
Making Her Cry
Crystallized frozen tears.
Daily Decorating the shivering silver grass.
With dainty delicate diamonds.

Inlying,
Your nose
Sticking out the blanket.
Caught with its pants down.
Feels like old Blue's nose.
Damp. Wet. Cold.

With choreographed lazy resistance.
You Give in & Gaze up.
Staring and staring at
Dimmed stars hiding in clouds.
Playing
Hide and seek with your pupils.

Showing
Slippery,
Sad Shadows,
Too shy

To say hello.

Early Dawn
Sits Alone Again.
Silent on the Edge of time.
Somewhere between the first & last Drowsy Dream.

This Maiden Sunrise Voyage
Holds precious cargo, "Slumber."
Brazenly Burglarized and Broken into bits
By a choir of Badass Blackbirds.
Performing live, loud & in living color.
Singing Solos. Singing two-part harmonies.
Creeping louder & louder in your ears.
Like when You first learned to whistle.

Premature Yawns are born."Ahhhh"
They connect like dots,
Stretching unawake arms
Into tangled bedsheets.

Brain cells slur bilingually…please, please
Por Favor. Por Favor.

Just one more minute. Just one more minute.
Un memento. Un memento.
Just 60 seconds more.
Of Blissful Beautiful,
Horizontal Retreat.

Early Dawn
Sits Alone Again.
Silent on the edge of time.
Somewhere between the first & last Drowsy Dream.

Suddenly,
Faster than Steph Curry's
Laser beam Buzzer Beater…
All you hear is "whoosh."
Lighthouse beams scream in your iris.
You blink.
&
The next thing you know…
Ear piercing aromas
Decode your favorite combo.
Black coffee. Strong enough to walk… home.
Alongside Mama's peaches & pancakes.
Words shake their heads.
"Uh uh uh."
&
Sit Down

Too tired
Of describing the taste.
Now, your nose starts yelling at your stomach,
Making it mad as hell.
Taste buds will be tap dancing.
On your tongue.
But.
Vision is Hot - Gun Glued Shut.

Double daring to open.
Passively Pulling apart
Lazy Lingering Lids.
Crack open like thin ice.

Just One quick peek.
Just One quick little peek
Finds hands standing at attention.

Six am Sharp, as a knife.
Tick Tock Time
Cuts Deep Down
Into your Semi-consciousness.
Slapping it twice (slap-slap)
Like some old raggedy
Cold wet towel.
"Get up."

Embury Avenue

Embury Avenue
Houses nestled with trees & sidewalks.
Every Early morning
Savory Smells drift through the seaside air.
Eggs & bacon breakfast.
Sometimes Cereal too.
You could smell whose house was cooking.

We would play outside
Seven days a week - 365.
Till the streetlights came on.
Snowball fights, marbles & playing jacks.
Jumping rope, running & hiding
& riding our bikes.

Our Street.
Our Family.
Houses nestled with trees & sidewalks.

Playing football with Larry and Gerald.
Robyn. The best at throwing & running fast.
Donnelly would talk us into anything.
Hiding from Kim so she wouldn't find us.
Going in that alley across the way.
Racing our bikes on dirt roads.
Poppin Wheelies.

Ridge Avenue was just down the road.

Always stopping at Lil's store
For candy & gum.
We ruled our School.
We walked & laughed & fought our way home.

Playing Basketball & Touch Football too.
Next steps... Jr. High & High School.
Those years flew by like...
Ice cream melting on a hot summers' day.
Neptune High v Asbury Park every fall.
The Red & Black v The Blue and Black.
We knew we had the best team,
Even when we lost.

Our Street
Our Family.
Houses nestled with trees & sidewalks.

We even had our own signal call.
"Hee Yock Key" "Hee Yock Key"
That was our call to come out and play.
Catching lightning bugs in a jar.
Climbing trees & scraped knees.
Summer hot nights sitting on the steps.
Waiting for the Ice Man to come
You could hear his music
Sometimes a mile away.

Beverly & Areatha lived next door.
Larry lived two houses away.

Enid & Gerald lived across the street.
Somehow,
We always played in our yard.
Making up our games on the spot.
Our Street.
Our Family.
Houses nestled with trees & sidewalks.

Our backyard was the biggest on the block.
One day a pool arrived.
But Nobody knew how to swim.
Splashing water everywhere.
We were the "coolest" kids
On Embury Avenue.

Our Street
Our Family
Houses nestled with trees & sidewalks

Houses gone; trees gone too.
If you close your eyes & smile.
Listen with your heart's eye.
You will hear us laughing & talking loud.
Our memories will hold on forever.
Our Street.
Our Family.
Embury Avenue.

Footsteps / Footprints
a poem for Mary Moore

This poem was one of the hardest poems I have ever written.
How do you put Mary Moore into words?
The press couldn't do it justice. Lois Pearlman's book created
community with the words of your past.
Telling your story with grace and grit.

Mary Moore...
It's not **what** you did, it's not **when** you did it.
It's not **where** you did it. It's not **how** you did it.
It's not **who** you did it with either.
It's **WHY** you did it. It's **WHY** you did it.
It's **W H Y** you did it.

All of us have morals, flaws, dreams.
All of us have compassion. And all of us have spirit.
Mary Moore has boldness tattooed on hers.

My Nerd
Came out and celebrated
The Deep Dive Discovery Research I did About You.
Leading me to a gentle woman named Lois Pearlman who
wrote your biography **Unfit Mother.**

And to a gentle man named
Peter Bryne. He wrote this about you...

Occidental Anarchist

"There once was a young Rebel named Mary
Whom The System viewed as Kontrary.
But try as They* might,
She's been shining her Light,
From the fairy-blessed Redwoods so airy
In a Tree House of Radical Art,
Festooned with Boxes of Proof
That It is
The System Itself that is Doomed
Not our Mary Full of
Grace, Not Exactly,
But more than Merry in Battles
Well Fought. Cross her not."
—Peter Byrne
This limerick lives in lasting love.

Mary Moore
Archangel Anarchist Activist
Continuously Celebrates her Life.
89 trips around our burning super star.
A life filled
With cups half full & cups half empty.
Drama lived at your doorstep leaving Cliff Notes life lessons.
You came.
You saw.
You challenged the Pillars of Bull Shit.
You Grabbed Fear by the Balls.
Tattooed with Scars of Controversy,

82

You Stood Tall.
You Spat in the Fucking Faces of Hypocrisy.
Herstory will tell your Truth.
Not the Courts,
Not the Media.
Not the Gossiping
Burning Lips of polluted plastic politicians.
Your Autobiography movie script genres
Defies nonfiction & fiction.
Spanning across
Documentary, comedy, drama,
adventure, action, tragedy,
Mystery, & don't forget romance.

Mary Moore
Your **footsteps** burned political discourse.
Your **footprints** lead to lasting liberation.
Your FBI file
Is still classified as a
Threat to National Security
With intent to Destroy & Overthrow the US gov't.
You took your Beauty Queen Cocktail Waitress days
And manifested, And created a conscious life where...
Critical Thought,
Radical Dissent,
Social & Political Revolution,
Nonconformity,
Created Liberation.

You ate Local & International

Conflict "Conflakes"
Not cornflakes for breakfast.
Living in a time of
Chaos and cataclysmic change.
All the Isms Ran. Ran Away Fast from you!
With fainting fear in their hearts.
Racism, Classism, Feminism,
Ageism, Ableism, Absolutism, and most of all Sexism.

Redefined by your activism and adventures.
Mary, did you know,
Bias & Prejudice
The Tragic Twins
Were looking for you today?

They loved cussing you out daily.
Threatened by your Redefined activism & adventures.
Did you know…
San Luis Obispo
Has an invisible statute of a
Nude White Woman in Birkenstocks
Fighting Patriarchal Powers.
Some say she looks a lot like you, Mary.

Imagine a woman with **Real** Power.
Real Courage.
With Glorious Guts & Outstanding Ovaries
Fighting for the **Real** Truth.
Redefining Activism.
Yesterday, Today and Tomorrow.

Any door that was closed. You burst through
Shedding light, love, and liberation.
Shattering Shadows of doubt,
Despair, division, & deceit.
No ceiling too high.
No voice too loud.
Voices Became Vocal Actions.
Your Legacy
Will live on.
Buried in Banned books of tomorrow.
Your Legacy
Will live in Songs
About "Pain-in-the-Ass-Sheros".
Your Legacy
Will live in Children
Remembering Russian River Memories
Of your Courage and Kindness.

Your Ancestors smiles
Silently slide across
Faces of Your Children.

Mary Moore.
Friendships come and go
Fearless Friendships live forever.
Mary Moore, your words say it all.
"The bottom line is
that all of us
who are working in
progressive politics

have a lot in common.
In terms of meaningful survival
there's a handful, of white men
Who are profiting off our miseries,
And it's time for us to
Join together and take a stand."

Mary Moore
You were born
With baby bird blue eyes Wide open.
You were born
With Fearless Fists Armed with truth, Courage. Stubbornness.
And Love.
Thank you for being one of the Badass "Real Ones."

We are thankful for your Birth
Let's Celebrate your Day.

The Royal Roast of Mary Moore

89 Trips around the Sun and now your first Royal Roast

1. Did you know Scientists discovered your fingerprints
On hundreds of DIY Tic Toks of
How to take the Government Down.

2. Is it true your file was
Destroyed for National Security purposes?

3. Is it true the US Government put
Your file in a Time Machine for 100 years for Safety?

4. Is it true the Secret Service have your phone number on
speed dial?

5. Is it true your file is in the Dark Cloud Floating somewhere
over Russia?

6. Some say your legacy is a tattoo of the Anarchy Symbol in
the Museum of Women's History.

7. Are you wanted in all 50 states & territories for Fighting for
Truth & Freedom?

8. Are your dreams banned in the new US history books?

9. Did The Last Poets write about you in 1969?

10. Is your birthmark invisible to those who Spin Webs of
Lies?

11. Is your land line phone still tapped today?

12. Is it true Four Former US Presidents swore to silence for
knowing your secrets?

13. Is it true we smoked weed in Johannesburg, South Africa?

14. Are the code words "Mary Moore" used as a discreet tactical antisocial strategy the CIA & FBI use for their trainings.

15. It is true, Mary, The Bohemian Grove has a price on your head for the next 100 years for ten million dollars?

16. Are you sure there aren't any Secret International Spies under cover here today?
If so, Welcome Mother Fuckers.

89 Trips around the Sun Mary Moore
You are revered and feared at the same time.
89 is just the beginning of your fearless journey to dismantle all the Isms all by yourself.

You taught us how to fight, create community, network, mobilize, strategize & meet, greet, and never retreat.
Taking a stand was your baby steps, Mary.
You walk & talk "Real Talk" with No Bull Shit.
You are the Standard, Mary Moore.
Your footsteps burned political discourse.
Your footprints lead to lasting liberation.
You not only worked for progressive politics,
You wrote the manual
And then gave it away to everybody you met.
Thank you for being
The Original O.G. of the Badass "Real Ones."

Goodnight. Goodnight Moon.

Home.
My Center.
My Roots.
My Seeds.
I Can't Tell One From The Other.
Home.
A Place InBetween
A Moment and a Miracle.
A Time Before We Were Born.
Home.
Grounded. Solid. Strong.

So…Listen.
Care
Fully.
I See Through You.
Cover Up Your Blank Spots.

Follow…
Your Musical Memories.
That Melody isn't stuck in your head.
It will find your way Home.

Follow…
Your Maze of Mysteries.
They will become Meaningful Mornings.

Follow…

Your Foot...Prints and Baby Steps
As they Cover Up and Say Goodnight.
Home.
I know the Way..
I know the Way...
Back...Home.

Welcome. Home.
Welcome. Home.
Home.

Graduation Poem

I have found that
Nothing
In Life
is
Worthwhile.
Unless…
you
take
Risks.

Nothing.
Absolutely Nothing.
Nada.

Nelson Mandala said,
"There is no passion
to be found
Playing Small."

Unless you are the *Golden State Warriors.*

He said,
*"There is **no** passion*
in settling in
Life
With less than
What you are
Capable of Living."

Less than
What you are
Capable of living.

So I say to you, today.
Fail Big.
Fail Big.

You **will** fail
More than once
in your life.

At some
Point
You **might**
Accept Failure as a Friend.

You **will** lose.
Sometimes Failure wins.
You **will** embarrass yourself.
We all do.
You **will** be last.
Not first.
No doubt about it.

The Flaws of Being Human
Incessantly insist on it.
Remember
Flaws.
Use Them.

Discover, Dissect, Deconstruct Them.

There is not one
Profession on this planet,
A class, nor a task.
That is
100%
Fail-safe.
When you
"Incorporate
Some feature
For the Purpose of
Automatically

Counteracting the effect
Of an anticipated
Possible Source
of Failure."

Graduates,
Be uncomfortable with uncertainty.
Be Uncomfortable
With Uncertainty.

Ask Questions.
Be Socratic. Ponder.
Look up at the stars and dream.
Look down at the dirt and dig.

Bask in the Beauty of Innocent Ignorance.

Imagine Healthy Homemade Lemonade smoothies.

Failure.
She is your Teacher.
Failure is…
A place to pivot from.
Accessories include,
Unlimited, Underrated Free Gifts.

Gifts
of Patience,
Self Care,
Intelligence,
Experience,
Endless Empathy, and more.
These gifts are value added.
More than any ordinary,
Simple "Same Old Same" success.

So,
Graduates
Be Glorious.
Be Generous.
Be Grateful.

Embody, Embrace the Essence of
All Truthful Treasures in life.
Remember Truth and Trust are Twins.
They will serve you well.
You, too

Will also
Serve
The Hard Knocks of your Future.

So. Persevere.
Be Accountable.
Be Responsible.
Be Human.
Be Glorious.

Serve with Faded Flaws and Sacred Scars.
They will make you **wise**
Beyond your years.
Remember.
Wisdom lasts forever.

The Hausa people from Nigeria believe
"There are **three** Friends in Life:
Courage,
Common Sense,
And insight.
I say, there is a **fourth** Friend in Life.
Wisdom.

Take Them
With you
On your many, many **journeys.**

They will serve you well.

Hog Mog and Buttons Poem

Ancestor Amina
Brenda Lynn Robinson
Hog Mog and Buttons
Cosmic chaos aflame
One tiny dust ignites N2
A single shining shooting star.

Lingers and lands
Right on Water Street
Minutes past midnight
One cold
Cloudless Columbus night.
Below Freezing chills
Crystalizing
DNA's burning embers
N2
Charcoal.
Radiant, vivid, vibrant colors
Even the blind could see
Bursting Breathtaking
Boiling Black Beauty
N2 living home made
Intricate,
intimate,
Intrinsic,
identic,

Observational Penetrations.
96

Observational Penetrations.

Slowly freeing each ancient secret gift
Buried deep deep in the
Young yoke of Sankofa's egg.

Masqueraded in Heavenly/Humanform
Introducing the one and only,
Ancestor Amina
Brenda Lynn Robinson.
1940
48 days old.

Born with
Mother's Nature
Father's wit
Born with
Keys of kindness, knowledge, Grace.
And
Homemade Hog Mog.

You know the recipe
Step 1
Libation for the ancestors
Step 2
Gather sticks for a fire.
Step 3
Cross **nine new needles twice.**
Step 4
Click your **thimble** 22 times.

Find the **oldest** pot.
Kiss it with **three** drops of hot sauce.

Add
One cup pig grease
From that can sittin on the stove.
One cup of paint (any old paint will do.)
One cup wet red mud
One cup **African Wisdom**
Boil, mix, stir to the rhythm of Coltrane.

Amina hears music **all** the time.
"Stories that were passed down to me **are musical."**

Amina sculpts imagines **N2** art.
Amina knows **how** not **why.**
She says **Art is not Art.**
Art is **Life.**
Life N2 Art
N2 Life. N2 Art
N2 Life N2 Art.

Remember.
"One's life does not
Begin **with** oneself."
"I stand on **their** shoulders."

Amina hears Ancestral Lullabies
Harmonizing Black **Soul stirring** Spirituals.

She sees **layers and layers** of timeless Sankofa.
She smells fish frying
Every Friday from some Down Home Honky Tonks.

She buttons the **essence** of Cosmic Meanings.
She time travels to Destiny 4am **everyday.**
She decodes signals **sent** centuries and centuries ago.
She cast dyes
On **stories** threaded 4
Ancestral robes.
She sews music boxes
N2 **quilts** with joy.

She Stitched Colors N2 Truth.
She Stitched Sounds N2 Kindness.
She Stitched Words N2 a **lifetime** of **Grace.**

Ancestor Amina
Brenda Lynn Robinson
Designs Destiny Maps
AKA
RagGonNons
Eternity's GPS.

**"It doesn't come out of me.
It comes through me."**

She is shaped by the power of **memory.**
Created with **one** purpose:
2 **give**

to the future
2 **give**
To the children's future
2 bring out the **Soul Train**
Of your family
2 secure the Heart &Soul
Of your community.
2 touch **Afro Futures.**
Born to **live** tomorrow.

Amina's Womenfolk
Wisdom whispers waterless words.
Each Quilt
Effortless
Elegant
Exquisite
Enduring,
Emphatic,
Electric
African Elixir.

So take a sip
Take a sip
Taste Unapologetically Black
On your lips.

Be Glorious Amina.
Be Glorious…
Be Black.

Home

We all share the Same. The same place.
The same Outer Space The same sky.

The same moon.
The same sun.
The same air.
The same water.
That washes away our tears and our fears.
We all share the same history.

The same futures.
The same yesterdays, todays, and tomorrows.
The same mornings and the same midnights.
We all share the same.
We all love.
We all dream.
We share the same nightmares and we share the same
daydreams. We share the same fears. The same failures.
The same hopes.

We all learn.
We all get lost and we all get found.
We all loose and we all win.
We all listen to the same sensational sounds of summers'
Hot and cool, cool, jazz.
Yes, you, you, and you.
We all share the same home.
Yes, you, you,

And those who aren't here at this moment
Yet, will live forever in our hearts.
We all have the same home.
The flora in the forests,
On the ocean floors
The most restless, relentlessly stubborn
Green wonder that grows inbetween
The cracks of everywhere.

Why? Why? Why?

Because we all share the same home
Look around,
Look around and see

See Your DNA in the eyes of
Your mother, your father, your sister, your brother.
Because.
We all share the same.

Home. A poem for Christopher Bowers

HomeMade Habitat.

The Place
Where Memories
Silently Sojourn.

Such Sanguine
Solitary Sanctuaries.

The Place
Where Your Feet's' On the Ground
Head In the Sky.

The Place.
Where you know
It's Okay.

The Place.
Where Remembering Resides.

The Place.
For Rhythmic Retreat.

Where The First Dreams dwell.
Where The First Echoes
Sing Your Favorite Songs.

That's Where I Want To Be.

Pick Me Up and Turn Me Around.

Where the first Aromas.
Dance and Move
Like Shadows
Chasing Themselves.

They pick and pick
As they perforate your Past.
Like Aunt Areatha's
Perfect Perfume.
All Ways Love.

Where the first Falls
Ins and Outs of Love
Again, and Again and Again.

Discovering and Falling in Love with
Full Moon Midnight Starry Nights.
Discovering and Falling in Love with
The Serene Surreal Sonoma Coast.
Discovering and Falling in Love with
Rylan's Magical Laugher.
Discovering and Falling in Love with
Brand New Guitar Strings.
Discovering and Falling in Love with You Got Light in Your
Eyes.

Home.
Heavy like

Massive Merciful Moons.

Light like
Vanishing Velvet Valentines.

Home.
Where the first Chills of October
Looks on Laughing
As the Last Leaf
Lingers and Lingers and Lingers
Knowing It Too
Must Fall
As We Drift In and Out.

Home.
I Love This Passage of Time.
To Finally Find...
Myself...
Back...
Home

Home.
Is My Heart.
Healed. Broken.
Home.
Where I Still See
The Light in Your Eyes.

Home.
Is My DNA.

Unstained. Unpolished. Unquestioned.

Home.
Where I Say
Goodnight. Goodnight Moon.

Home.
My Center.
My Roots.
My Seeds.
I Can't Tell One From The Other.
Home.
A Place InBetween
A Moment and a Miracle.
A Time Before We Were Born.
Home.
Grounded. Solid. Strong.

So... Listen.
Care
Fully.
I See Through You.
Cover Up Your Blank Spots.

Follow...
Your Musical Memories.
That Melody isn't stuck in your head.
It will find your way Home.

Follow...

Your Maze of Mysteries.
They will become Meaningful Mornings.

Follow...
Your Foot...Prints and Baby Steps
As They Cover Up and Say Goodnight.
Home.
I know the Way..
I know the Way...
Back...Home.

Welcome. Home.
Welcome. Home.
Home.

Home. We Share the Same.

Home
We All Share the Same.

The Same Place. The Same Outer Space. The Same Sky.
The Same Moon. The Same Sun.
The Same Air.
The Same Water. The Same Tears & Fears.

We All Share the Same.

History.
The Same Futures. The Same Yesterdays. Todays &
Tomorrows. The Same Unknowns. The Same Mornings. The
Same Midnights.

We All Share the Same.

We All Love. We All Dream.

We Share the Same. Nightmares. Daymares.

We Share the Same Fears.

The Same Failures. The Same Hopes.

We All Learn the Same.

We All Get Lost. We All Get Found. We All Lose. We All Win.
We All Listen

To the Same Sensational Sounds Of Summer. Weary Winds
Of Winter.

We All Get Hot. We All Get Cold. We All Feel Jazz Deep in
Our DNA.

Yes.
You.
You and I
Are the Same. Hiding
Deep
Inside Shared Shameful Histories.
We Share the Same. Families... Friends... Enemies... Lovers...

We Are All the Same.

We All Live
On the Same Planet. Breathe the Same Air. Drink the Same
Water. Bleed the Same Blood.

Eat the Same Food. Smile When We Laugh. Feel the Same
Pain. Cry the Same Tears.

Hope the Same Dreams. Share the Same Future. Share the
Same Past. Share the Same Present.

We Are All the Same.

We All Live. We All Die.

We All Share the Same.

Home. Mountains. Deserts. Flora.

Forests.
Fauna. Oceans.
Large & Small.
We All Share the Same.

Housed & Houseless.

We Change. We Grow.

Like Restless, Relentlessly Stubborn DNA.

We Share the Same DNA Wonders Like
Twins & Pineapple
Jazz & Birthmarks
Brown eyes & Daisies.

That grows In-between the cracks
Of Every Sidewalk We Share.

Look
In the Mirror. See
The Eyes of Your Mother. Your Father. Your Sister. Your
Brother. See. Your Smile On Their Face.

We Are All The Same. Welcome Home. Again.

HomeComing a Poem for Ann Gray Byrd

HomeComing Holds
Encapsulated Memories,
Bronze Ebony shines shadowless,
Leaving jealous shade
Playing Hide and Seek.
Air Blushes
With the scent of her
Very first Kiss.
Glimmering at first,
Then glowing warmer, warmer Deep down in between
Oxygen Onyx.

Sista Queen Sirens sit
At her feet and Sing Steadfastly.
Silent Echoes Ending
Soulful Sojourn Sorrows.
Hear them Hum.
Yes, They Hum.
Humming so smooth, Thousands & Thousands
Of Honey Bees freeze in Midair. Humming in Heavenly
Harmony.

Listen, Only
Your Heart Ears can hear.
Trembling, Trembling Trembling Voices.
Her Voice Too.
Memories Melt. Memories
Mesmerized

In the corner of your Eye.
In the back of your head.

She...
Cakewalks, Strolls,
Straight Up Struts.
Effortlessly Electric Slides
Smiling in Silence, She dances.
Smiling in Silence, She sings,
She Laughs, and She lives,
Right in the middle of your Third Eye.

Bond Safely for Eternity, Endless
Yesterdays were born.
Each Ornate, Each Ancient, Each African.
BlackBlood codes cut paths on their journey.
While Motown Melodies
Loudly play on the car radio.

Her secret codes reveal
Mysteries and Miracles.
Each Code set inside
Blood Diamonds encrypted
with A Precious Pattern
Somewhere in Sankofa's Timeless Time.

Yesterday's Ring Out Loud
Glorious Gales kiss
Gentle Breezes
Syncopated Scats Sing Downwind
Into your Backdoor Kitchen Window.

Clarity. Consciousness.
Like a Sudden Rain in Early Sonoma Spring.

Walk down any street in South Park,
Listen to her giggling echoes.
They Laugh and Dance with you.
She is waiting.
We are waiting.
HomeComing.
ComingHome.

Homecoming Holds

Homecoming
Holds
Encapsulated Memories,
Bronze Ebony shines shadowless,
Leaving jealous shade
Playing Hide and Seek.
Air blushes
With the scent
Of her very first kiss.
Glimmering at first,
Then glowing warmer.
Warmer
Deep down

Imagine
This poem is dedicated to Bessie Smith

Imagine A Black Universe Of Love, Sex,
And the Blues.

Imagine.
Black Owned EVERYTHING. From Honky Tonks to
Hospitals. From Night Clubs to Night Schools.

With Lots and Lots and Lots Of Ladies Living Large
AND NOT FREE.

Imagine.
A Black Universe.
AKA
The Harlem Renaissance. Emerged slowly one Summer hot
early sunrise morning. After a long, long drought
And Midnight Lightning Storm.

The Harlem Renaissance. Young. Gifted. Black. Radical.
Revolutionary. Romantic. Refreshing.
Rich. Real. Rare.
AND NOT FREE
This Ebony Universe existed During the Willie Lynching
Years. 1920's. 1930's. 1940's. 1950's.
AND NOT FREE.

There's only one way to travel around This Onyx Universe.
Your Green Book GPS Guide.
The First Black GPS in the history Of the United States of

America.
AND NOT FREE.

Some Say, This Black Universe
Was Delightfully Dark.
Dense. Deep with Sensual Shooting Stars. Chocolate Milky
Ways.
Graceful Grandiose Galaxies. Sacred Soulful Suns.
And Star Dust.
Star Dust Everywhere.
AND NOT FREE.

Populated with Pulsating Planets. Colored Comets & Musical
Meteors. Millions & Millions of
Magic Mama Musical Moons. Full Moonlight Was So Silently
Soft It Slowly Melted Cut Crystal
In a Whisper.
AND NOT FREE.

Imagine.
Bessie Smith Arrives
Super Nova Shooting Star
On This Jet Black, Achromatic Universe.
AND NOT FREE.

Foot stomps on the stage. Shadows Scatter.
Spotlights burn bright.
Honey Black Brown Renaissance Royalty.

Crowned Empirical Empress Of the Blues,

Cross Dressing Daring Diva, Color Line Crossing, Motherless
Memories, Fatherless Fatigue, Fearless Feminist, Limitless
Lovers, Survivor of Violence, And The Great Oppression.
AND NOT FREE.

Imagine. Bessie Smith Mentored by
The Queen of the Blues. Miss Ma Rainey.

Bessie & Ma Were like Frankie & Johnnie. No Love Lost there.

That Union created One of the many Black G.O.A.T.S. & Sheep
of The Harlem Renaissance.

Bessie Smith became
The Greatest of All Time Blues Singers
AND NOT FREE.

She sang. "Trouble, Trouble, Trouble. I had it all my days.
"It seems like Trouble. Going to follow me
To my grave."

Oh No. No.
No grave will ever hold you, Bessie Smith.

Your voice moved millions

To fall in love with the Blues.

Your "Stand Your Ground" Courage Shadowed the #MeToo
Movement Today
And

Tomorrow.

Thank You
Miss Bessie Smith.
For Being One of the **Real Ones**.

AND NOT FREE.

Imani

Imani

Means…
"God is with us."

Swahili for…
Faith.
Trust.
Belief.
Peace.

Imani.

Zulu for…
Belief.
Faith.
Sweet EZ
Tribal constructs
Sharing Black Mysteries.
Black Ancient Ancestral Wisdoms.
Black Intelligencia.

Disguised as Language
Of our Ancestors.
Humming. Humming
Incessantly in ours ears…

Jazz, flowing into Blues.

Blues swaying into Gospel.
Gospel swooning deep
Down Dark Deep
Down
Under
Black Diamond Designs.
Moaning and Knowing.

Balsamic Black Universe.
Black Grapes from Black Wine
Taste bittersweet on our tongue.
Taste
Inside the bitter.
Inside this Blackness.
For "The Blacker the Berry..
The Sweeter....the wine."
Taste.
Kaleidoscopic Concave Blackness
Balsamic Black Shadows shades
Linger with Indigo
Afterglows.

Aurora Borealis
Shine from Deep Down
Dark Draped Cobalt Black
Moonless Skies.

Imani

120

"God is with us"
Four Super Power Words.
"God."
"Is."
"With."
"Us."

GOD. (Let's talk about God)

God is…
Faith.
OG Belief.
Based on Faith and Belief.
On Faith and Belief.
Faith and Belief.
Generational Daydreams and Nightmares.
Woven with blood stained fingers
Hidden in the quilts of enslaved Africans.
Faith and Belief.
Infinite.
Convictions
Of Trust.
Infinite.
Indiscriminately infinite
Just look around and see…
The Faces of Faith.
Faith **is God.**
God is Faith.

Standing Strong
Like Soweto
Children Warriors
Ready at the quick.

Imani

IS (Let's talk about is)
My favorite word **is...is**
For me
It "**is**"
The Glue.
The Bridge
The Present Tense.
"You **Is**..."
"I **is**..."
"We **is**..."
"God **is.**
Infinitely....Clear.

Ancient knowledge
Falls from our
Dreams like... stardust.
You hear.
You see.
You feel.
You know
You **is. Real.**

Imani

Middle English says
Is means
Equal.
That Meaning is not true.
NO.
We **is** not equal.
We **is**…
Struggling in Eye of the Storm.
We **is**…
Surviving in the Eye of the Storm.
We is here.
We is now.
Yesterday and tomorrow.
Always and Forever.
In the Eye of the Storm.
Some say…
We **is**
"The Eye of the Storm."

IS
God is.
Love **is.**
Faith **is.**
Black **is.**
We **is.**

Imani

DNA Destiny Drops
Invisible vapors

Drizzle Detailed Desires
Wet and Real.

WITH.
Around **us.**
On **us.**
In **Us.**
Us.
With us.

(Let's talk about **with**)
"With" means…
Accompanied by…
Possessing something…
"It **is with** me."
In relation to.
"She **is with** child"
In the same direction as…
"Come **with us.**"
Us.

Us. (Let's talk about Us)
We is us.
Bound.
Inseparable.
Undeniable.
Unapologetically
Us.
You know Us.

Now take these four little words
"God Is With Us."

Whisper them
Inside that timeless,
Tiny, Tattered Teacup
Mama never threw away.
Let it go.
Feel it
Fly far, far away…

This vow.
This declaration.
This assurance.
These four words.
This Secret Code.

"God is With Us."

Signals…

Infinite waves of Life.
Resistance. **P**ersistence.

Infinite Waves of **B**lackness.
Love. Honor. Trust.

Infinite Waves of **B**lack **G**race.
Compassion. Dignity. Integrity.

Infinite Waves of **B**lack Faith.
Beyond Faith. Beyond Faith.

Imani.

Forever and Ever.

Imani.

Kwanzaa is not just once a year.
We carry Imani
In the DNA Drizzle Drops of Destiny.
Carry them.
On and on and on.

Imani

In the Cool Calm Air

A single
Layer
Of molecules
Each HoldingHands to survive.
Sankofa's
Cold, clear stares.
Each
Hand holds…
Calm Captive Memories,
Homemade Hidden Hopes,
Daydreams of the Dead.
Each Hand.
Indigo Inked
With Iceberg Cold
SweetTea.

Tea. So Cold,
Your can't feel your fingers
When they touch.
Each hand
HummingandHopingandHolding
Millions and millions
Of melted
Mystical MajesticMemories.
Follow the path of memories
InnerVisions Awaits.

Follow the path of memories
InnerVisions Awaits.
All Clear.
All Seeing,
All Knowing,
All Being
Inside
All
The Universes
Smiling inside your Eyes.

Night vision
Blurred by echoes
Tangled in webs&young vines
Dressed In Mint Green Spring
Lingering from
The first Poplar tree.
Faded Footprints say... **Run.**
Run **Far Far away.**
Chased by blood shadows
Of yesterday's nightmares
And pregnant daydreams.
They say, "Run. Run Fast.
Run To Run To
Distant Deflowered Whispers
Singing Siren Stolen Songs.
Singing
Fly. Yes, Fly.
Like Golden Gentle Gales
Fly like…

Warm Winter Wisdom on
Wings of Wind."

Signaling, sending
Connecting and connecting
And connecting
Crystal Clandestine
Coded morning messages.
Like some song stuck in the back of your head
From yesterday's yesterdays.
Well, my friend,
StarLings. Know.
They know That song.
That same song
Stuck in the back of your head.
Iridescent Feathers of Knowledge
Black Wisdom on Wings.
StarLings
FearlesslyFly
with seven dots
Of stardust on Their Wings.
Galactic GPS's.
AI can't even touch.

And don't forget
Don't forget…to
Look fast,
Before you blink,
Before you think.
Before you sleep.

They will fly
Into your dreams.
And Sing.
Long Lovely Lullabies.
Long Lovely Lullabies.
Lullabies are MemoryMelodies.
Lullabies are MemoryMelodies.
Melodies inMotion
Are
Murmurations.
Murmurations.
Miracles in Motion.
Intricate. Intimate.
Kaleidoscopic Patterns,

Delicately detailed,
Delightfully, determined
Destiny Designer Designs.
Painted Water Wet with
Invisible. Invincible.
Identic.
Iceberg Colors.
Tinting Cloudless Skies
With ten thousand
Paintless Rainbows.
Such Majestic,
MagicalMarvels.
Dancing DNA.
Dancing DNA.

Dancing.
Flying.
Soaring.
Dreaming.
Being.
In the
cool
calm
air.

Invisible Identities

333 years ago
1690 was the year.
John Locke wrote.
"The necessity of pursuing
Happiness
Is
The **Foundation**
of Liberty."

The **Foundation**
of Liberty.

Liberty is:
The State
of **not** being
In confinement
or Servitude.

Liberty.
Freedom.
Manumission.

Liberty.
The Mother of Human
Inalienable Rights.
Inalienable
To Life
To Liberty.

To Property.

Locke's Words
Warmly Whispered
In the Wise Winter Wind.
Wandering
Into the ears of 21 children.

As brave as 11 years wise.
Children From
Mountains, Cities, Forests, Islands,
Farms,
From across America.

They all walk on the same path.
Wearing different shoes.

Children Authors of
A **New** Social Contract.
From A
New Age of Enlightenment.
Creating
New Song to Save the Planet.

Singing a **New**
Global Harmony.

Voices
interconnecting.
Intersecting.

Interchanging.

Voices
Becoming
Brave.
Courageous
Stewards of Humanity.
In service to
Every Human's Right
on
Planet Earth.

Stewards of
Human Rights Issues
From
Millions of
Domestic / International
Marginalized Communities.
Underserved & Served.

Activists all asking about.

Our Climate Crisis.

Our Gender Inequity Crisis.

Our Educational Crisis.

Our Migrant Rights Crisis.

Our Social Economic Crisis.

Our Future Crisis.

So STOP!
PLEASE STOP!

Close your eyes.
Imagine.

Millions and Millions
Of **invisible Identities**.
Stewards of Humanity
In Service to Our
Economic, Civil, Social Justice.
In Service to Our
Gatherings from Grassroots to Global.
In Service to Our
Compliance to all Compassionate Communities.

Stewards of Humanity.
Let's
Say their Names.
Say their names today.

Steward Advocates such as…

Vivek, Keley, Julia, Mel, Camille,
Ana, Mulika, Hunayn, Sofia,
And so many many more.

The future has a fighting chance
When you are fighting for our future.

An Old African Hausa proverb says,

"There are three Friends
In life.

Courage,
Sense,
And insight.

Stewards of Humanity
Stewards of Human Rights.

May your friendships last a lifetime.

I Pledge

I pledge allegiance to the Flag
Of the United States of America.
And to the republic
For which It stands,
One Nation.
Under God.
Indivisible.
With Liberty.
And Justice for All.

Why do I know this ?
Why do I know every word without thinking about it ?

Is it because we've deconstructed and unpacked this concept
In our laboratories of learning as young lambs?
Or somewhere on silent segregated streets ?

Is the ease and flow of these particular words
As Effortless as its' meanings or understanding?
Do wc walk the talk?

Has the United States of America
Pledged its' ideology to me?
If you know the answer...
Please allow the learning process to evolve.
I willfully and soberly
Pledge
My allegiance to

Our Ideology
to the Ideals of the people
Of the United States of America
For which they have always stood.
Today. Tomorrow. Yesterday.

Are we not a republic ?
Are we not a state where our
Supreme power is held
By those we elect
To represent us?

Are we not a electorate?
To elect a president

And not a monarch.
I don't mean the butterfly.
Let the law of the land reflect the intentions of the people.

We can amend the Constitution of the
United States of America
To pledge directly and honestly
To the masses
To the millions and millions of
Unapologetic individuals.

Each as different as…

Loud and silent and those not heard
As different as Day and Night.

And those In-between.
As different as you and me and those unseen.
As different as Left, Right, Center, and those who reside in the margins.

Are we not one diverse nation?
A nation conceived from places all around the world.

I pledge to the People of the USA.
Has the people of the United States of America pledged to herself?
We therefore, Proudly, Patriotically Pledge to ourselves.

Are we not aware that we are the republic?
We are the ones who hold collective and individual power.

Is one world nation enough?

God and Politics are bitter bedfellows.

They don't talk to each other anyway.
How would the multilingual voices of God converse with
The polygon voices of our politic?

So.
Stop.
Visualize a nation of unapologetic individuals.

United.
Healing.

I W D Poem
International Women's Day

I W D
International Women's Day
One Day
One Woman
One World.

One + One + One
Equals minus One.
$1 + 1 + 1 = (-1)$

51% of the Human Species.
<76% of the Living Wage.
100% of All Yesterdays, Todays and
Tomorrow.

24 Hours...Everyday, Everyday, Everyday
Countless duties.
Countless hours, minutes, days
Countless Decades of Unfulfilled Destinies
Disguised as Dreams.

Each hour on Earth
A Woman is
Giving...Birth
Growing...Food. Children.
Grasping that Greedy Glass Ceiling.

Granting Wishes and Promises.
Glowing, Gazing, into the Unknown Future.
Governing, Getting Fucked.
Gathering, Guiding, Gardening,
Gifting, Gigging, to make ends meet.
Gaining more & more without Gravity.
Gliding, Grieving, Lost & Regrets
Going & Going & Going Mad.

IWD
International
Inter – Intra – Intro.
Into Nation States
Borderless Bound
With Betrayals & Birthmarks.

W
Women
Walk – Climb – Soar
On Land, Air,
And International Seas
Beyond All Political Definitions

Why? Why? Why?
Because
364 Days of the Year
We Are Invisible.

Today,
We See Ourselves.

Today,
We Sing. We Shout.
Beyond Time Zones.
Today,
We Make Herstory.

Today & Everyday
We Shatter those Mirrors
That Reflect Polluted Political Patriarchy.
That Pontificately Projected Prolific
Broken Promises.

Today.
Face to Face.
We Mirror the Future.
Every…Day.
Every…Woman.
Every…Where.
Look at Us.
Look at Us.
See Sankofa
Slide across our Smiles.

Jazz@Home

Single Moments Cloaked in Solitude.
Whispering Slowly Sliding
Slithering Softly
Singing. Soliciting.
Secretly In My & Miles' ears...

Minor Major Moments
Fall effortlessly into a place.
So precise. So perfect.
We Forgot We Remembered
One Musical Magical Memory
From not so long ago.

Waning Whispers
Echoes into Full Blown Gale of Sounds.

Some call Jazz.
Some call Black Music.
Some call
My Music.

Strong. Patient.
Poetic Pauses.

So Silent.
So Soft.
So Steadfast.
So Delicious.

Like Bill Evan's kisses.
Touching.
Tickling.
Tantalizing.
Tones.

You Taste in your Daydreams.

Soulful Solitude.
Slows the Sad.
Simple & Saucy.
Sorrowful & Suede.
Sexy Sweet & Savory.

So So Sweet.

So So Sweet.

Melting Moments.
Whispering In Each
Others' Ears.

Jazz & John Handy

The Harlem Renaissance of the West
Had Two Kings.
"King Jazz" & "King John Handy."
Both Born in the Western Kingdom of The Harlem
Renaissance
In San Francisco, California.
King Jazz was first on the scene.
Later came this Cat on sax called John Handy.
Musical Genius from Dallas.
He "busted his chops" by age 15.
His sound was so strong,
You could hear him jam
way across the bridge from Oakland.
Unaware of his Royal Artistry.
The Future of Jazz was shaped by his Humble Hands
& Tender Tones.
King Jazz and King John Handy literally
played together in
Clubs that still celebrate
The John Handy Quintet.
Echoes of his slow sax solos.
Leaving Projections of a Rainbow in...
The Fillmore. The Half Note.
The Both/And. Bop City and many more.
To become Majestic Memories.
In the Kingdom of the Harlem
Renaissance of the West.

King John Handy
Put his "Foot in the Bay Area Jazz Scene
& Beyond."
Dropping knowledge from
San Francisco State University,
To Carnegie Hall.
These Two Kings recorded together
Blending the "Cool"
San Francisco fog with the "Hot"
Black and Blues of Oak Town.
Add a cup of Down-home Dallas Delicious
Funk & Soul. Signature "Hard Work."
Charles Mingus and King John Handy recorded
"Live from Monterey Jazz Festival"
Classic Consummate Jazz.

Rolling Stone's Ralph Gleason
saw John Handy at
The Berkeley Jazz Festival.
He said, "It was one of the Great moments of
A Lifetime of listening to jazz."
King John Handy & King "Jazz" are Synonymous.
You filled us with Musical Love
For decades and decades.
Your overflowing gifts Are legendary.
History knows your name.
King John Handy
Of the Harlem Renaissance of the West.
Your Legacy will Lead us
Into the Future of Jazz.

Jazz Speaks for Life

"Jazz speaks
For Life."
"Blues tells
Their stories.
Sad, Sacrificing,
Sacred, Secret,
Strategic Successes.
Fragments From Life's Difficulties.

Musical Triplets
Jazz, Gospel, Blues
First cousins to Mama Africa.

Middle Passage passengers.
Poised praying,
Passionate possibilities.

They took the hardest,
Heaviest hateful realities,
Put them
into, in through,
inside, inbetween,
incised intimacies.

Simmered slowly
In Septembers' Summer sun.
Marinating magnificent,
Mathematical mysteries.

Blown through
Ancient temples of Tones.
Soul stirring saxophone solos.
Hummed into
Daydreamers dreams of Freedom.
Ghostly Guttural Groans
Lost Spirits sung.
Birthed into
Hearts of Jazz GOATS
Today, yesterday, and tomorrow.

Cut from
Grandpa Buster's
Cotton cloth pockets.
Leggetha's wise
Warm, worn
Quilts hiding maps
Stuffed with seeds
From stolen dreams
They all followed
North Star's path.

Stardust fell
On their heads.
Tracing footsteps and fear.

They made minds clean,
Clear, creative, conscious.
Miles, Coltrane, Ella,
Maya, Ta-Nehisi, Duke, and Destiny.

"They took Life
Offering no order
No meaning.
They created
Order Meaning
From the sounds
Through their instruments."

Imagine developing a
Critical mindset
Beliefs, Values,
Attitudes, Orthodoxies
Through the eyes of Sankofa.

Modern Jazz
Continues this timeless tradition
Singing songs from
More Complicated,

Contradicted,Confused
Urban existence.

"Change does not roll in
On wheels of inevitability,
But through continuous
Challenge and Controversy."

The Revolution was not televised.
She was in the recording studios.

Leaving Fingerprints
On wax, tape,
And digital dreams.

Bringing Bags
And Bags of Beats.

"New Hope
With a
Sense of Triumph.
Some call,

"Triumphant Music."

Some say,
Steppings stones
Into tomorrow.
Infused voices
Waiting to be heard.

Some say
To Be
Young
Educated.
Gifted.
Multicultural,
with
Ethnic Integrity.

The Future looks
Into the eyes
Of tomorrow.
She knows
Shadows of the past
Would soon fade.

JessicaJazz

JessicaJazz

Concise Connections.
Networking Notes.
Rhythms Fly
On Backs of Whimsical
Wicked Winds.

That's *JessicaJazz.*

Sax Solo Soars
into Your Soul.

Playing Hide & Seek
With Eternity...

Billy Higgins.
Soweto
Free Jazz.
Hard Hitting Bop.

Charles Lloyd.
Avant-Garde
Mystical.
Forest Flowers
Planted Forever.

Marcus Shelby.
Blues & Jazz Orchestral Magic.
Meditations on Dr. Martin Luther King, Jr.

Tiffany Austin.
Soulful Siren
Unbroken.

And Countless.
Countless More...
Syncopated Soldiers in
JessicaJazz's
Musical Army.

Proudly Pour
Their Hearts Out.
Playing Pure Patterns
of Sacred Sankofa.

That's **JessicaJazz.**

Young Minds
Meld
Into
Old Ones.

Touched
By Magic.

Disguised as
Musical Notes.

In-Between
Harmonies.
Decode Them.
Feel Them.
See Inside Them.

Practice.
Practice.
Practice.
Religious Repetitions.

Patterns
Punctuate
Pure
Power.

That's *JessicaJazz.*

She sees
Far
Into
Futures.

She Hears
Echoes Endlessly sing...

JessicaJazz.
JessicaJazz.

Juneteenth Ancestors are African

Juneteenth was born
Three minutes past midnight.
One
Hot, cloudless morning
After Eighteen sunsets in June.
Place: Galveston, Texas.
Year: 1865.

Juneteenth Ancestors are African.
Her story begins in Africa.
She Herself is
African and American.

She is one of the original **O.T's.**
Oldest Triple.
Sisters Trauma and Beauty are identical.

They hang from Poplar trees
All over & across the South.

Juneteenth Parents,
Grandparents, and Great Grandparents,
Lived to be over 400 years old.

She wears her mother's
Dark Smoldering Smoke-Stained Skin.

Scarred with warm memories and cold reality.
Juneteenth isn't
Her real name.
She is known by many names.
Freedom, Liberation, Revolution. Joy.

She has daydreams and nightmares
At the same time.
She Chases
sunbeams
Of Justice
And **slippery Shadows**
Of Freedom.

Juneteenth.
Onyx Oxymoron.
Mysterious and misunderstood.
Delicately. Delivering Destiny's' Dreams.

She sings songs to tomorrow's children.
Long Lingering Lamenting Lyrics
wet with
Buster Banging Beats of Enslavers' Nightmares.
Moaning Musical Melodies of Malcolm and Mahalia.

Juneteenth **Exists.**
Just Imagine…
Thousands and Thousands of
Terrifying Tortured
Tangled **Entrapments**

Along
Survivor less
Barren shores.

She Knowingly Knocked down
The **Door of No Return.**
Cape Coast Castle.
Ghana, West Africa.

Her African Ancestors
Are as **Real.**
As the nose on my face.
Hiding Miracles in Melanin.

Creating a World **from** Broken Promises.
Surviving a World **of** Broken Promises.

Juneteenth **jokes** of justice and freedom.
She **studies** Secrets in Shooting Stars
She **speaks** lost languages and Afro Futures.
Octavia Butler knew her cousin.

She walks in
Secondhand shoes
Too tight to feel safe.

Juneteenth is real. Y'all.
Juneteenth is alive.
She lives covertly
In-between pages of forgotten history.

She was conceived on bloody hemp
As General Order #3.
Etched in Ice Cold indigo ink.

She is an American Legal Decree
Issued 159 years ago.
Enforcing the Echoes of Emancipation
To the residents of the
U. S. state of Texas.
Freeing
Yes, FREEING.
F R E E-ING.
All Remaining
Enslaved Peoples
Forever.
AKA
"Leftovers" from
POTUS's White Tie
Dinner Party. Two years in the shade.

Juneteenth ended
So called "legal slavery".

But before she was born.
The USA was sick and suicidal.
Worshiping death and destruction
For **4** long years.
She fought in
The Civil Less War
The Black and White

Blood Brothers War.
Tracking misery hounds
Across her flower garden.

The Rest is history…Well.
Except in **22 states…like Florida.**
We keeps it *Real* in **California.**

She is the first
African American Federal Holiday
Born **from** Slavery directly into Jim Crow.

Today, We Remember **Her.**

Today, Yesterday and Tomorrow.

Remember **All** of her Dreams.
Remember **All** her Destroyed Destinies.
Remember **All** her Names.
Remember
She is
Buried in Unmarked Graves
Under Tomorrows' Tombs.
Trembling with Truth.

So, when you hear the name
Juneteenth
Remember to
Listen with your Third Eye.
Listen with your First Heart.

Wisdom is Whispering.
Wisdom is Whispering.

Whispering from
Sankofa's Bittersweet Smiles.

The Ancestors are listening...
The Ancestors are listening...

They know.
They know
Who & What
You are, Juneteenth.

History knows your Stories.
Ancestors know your Truth.

Remember,
Slaves did not come
From Africa.
Oh no. Slaves did not come
From Africa.
Teachers, Poets, Healers, Farmers, Architects,
Philosophers, Mathematicians, Scientists, Artists,
Men, Women,
Children, Human Beings
Came from Africa.

Life: A Poem

Before.
Before Mother Nature
And Father Time
Shared their
Intimate, Intricate Instruments.

Before.
Before Ageless Wisdom
Wrinkled by whispers of colorless centuries.

Served the last Griot
Sacred Tea and Secrets
Foretelling miracles touched by dirt
Echoing
The arrival of
The Original Omega.
The first Alpha.
The first Beta.
The first Ancestral Births.
Two Timeless
TruthTwins.
AKA. Love and Beauty.

Both Born Before.
Before
Sunrise and Sunset.
Oppositely Identical.

Each Baring seeds of
Daydreams and Nightmares.

Each Flying
Concentric Circles
Around and Around
Forests of FiveForevers.

Some**Time**
Between Shooting Stars
and Yesterday.
SomeWhere between Seven Spaceless Galaxies of untold
futures.

Love and Beauty.

Two Timeless
TomorrowTwins.
Creators with Ultimate Sacred Purity.

Our first Ancestors.
Both Birthers of Life.
Endless Ebony
Essence of Eternal Ecstasy.
Endless Ebony
Essence of Eternal Ecstasy.

Cardinal Knowledge Became Universal.
Their StarDust DNA.

Freedom freed
Their first MemoryMuscle.

Breath.

Exhale & Inhale.
Defiantly, Dangerously Dance with Desire.

Suddenly sliding in the Shadows
Watching and Waiting.
Watching and Waiting.
Waiting on the edge of eternity
Waiting to cut in?
Disguised in Voyeur skin and Blue Suede shoes.

Change. Change.
Continuous Colorless Change.
You **all** know her name.
Change.
<u>Octavia Bulter Parables</u>
<u>Fortold her Future.</u>
Change is **God.**
God is Change.

She Sleeps in Squined Shadows
South of Seven Secrets.

Her Seven Silent Secrets
Sing inside Sleeping Siren Songs.

Her Magenta Mysteries Become
Millions & Millions of Murmurations.

Her Murmurations Masquerade
As Mystical Muse Mysteries.

Overwhelming
Never Ending.

Ending Never
Her Reckless Love.
Her Reckless Life.
Her Cosmic Climatic Essence

Expels into Everyday Eternities.

Transformations

Tap Dance before your eyes.

Love Becomes Life.
Life Becomes Love.

Fear Becomes Invisible.

Invisible Became Fear.

Grace Becomes Omnipotent.
Omnipotence Became Grace.

All Seeing.
All Dreaming,
All Being.

All Becoming.

Her Beginning Forever.
Her Forever Beginning.

Ancestral.

Muddy Multifarious,

Handmade Miracles

Plant
DreamSeeds and DayDreams.

Plant
Wordless Speaking.

Plant
Endless Angelic Prayers.

Echoing, Echoing, Echoing.
Endlessly Echoing.

Love is Life.
Life is Love.

Love is Life.
Life is Love.

Never Ending
Ending Never.

Plant
Ancient Futures.
Futures Ancient.

Plant
Sowed Seeds Secretly.

Soon after
SankofaBegetsSankofa.

Life is Love.
Love is Life.

Interstellar.

Incessant.

Incarnate.

Life is Love.

Love is Life.

And So Much More.

166

Listen

Come Near.
Your daymares are nightmares.
Your nightmares walk Round lik strong Black coffee.
You dare not look back,
You keeps yo hed down
Ah dares you ta die today.

Listen
You hears dat wind blowin so mad?
Each leaf iz cussin her out fo it hits dah ground.
You hands so col
You fingers don't know
Each others when deh touch.

You eyes sees tomorrows an yesterdays.
Eyes sees so sharp, deh cut glass on a moonless nite.

Listen
You hear dat old crow? Singin da death song?
Every single moment, iz jugglin life or ded.
Life... Ded... Ded... Life.

She singin, "Whos gonna die todah?
Whos gonna die todah?
You dares not die todah!"

Listen Listen, Now
You hears dat hummin song
Stealin a ride on dah backs of dat breeze?
Da Sunset sings it to dah Sunriz.
She singin...
"What kinds of Ancestors yous gonna be?
What kinds of Ancestors yous gonna be?"

Your col feet dance like new shoes
Gigglin wit a secret.
Your heart too happy to beat...
Your drumbeat iz yo heartbeat.
Drumbeat... Heartbeat.
Heartbeat... Drumbeat.
You knos it.
You knos its
Way fo you born.

Listen
Dah first times I knos my reals blood names.
I hears it ins a dream whisperin loud insides me.
I hears it way fo my Mama was born.
My ears sees it.
My eyes hears it
My backs evens knos it.

Study longs on my backs.
Looks Close. My backs iz dah map.
Follow dah **Misery Map.**
Touch deeps down.

You fingers gently kiss ins-betweens dah scars.
Dey tells my Story. Dey spells my Name.

Your fingers follow dah misery.
Cuts deeps into those
Painful Paths. Follow. Find dat familiar first scar.
It knos. It knos.

Listen
Silence sound like o' ded trees.
Dey ain't silent. Dey Whisperin...
"Come Home, Come Home"
"Come Home To dah Promise Land"

Der iz no times. No pains.
No tears. No shames.
Come Home to dah Promise Land.

Yous Life iz Yours. Not Hiz.
Yous Body iz Yours. Not Hiz.
Yous Babies iz Yours. Not... Hiz.
Yous Soul iz Yours. Not Hiz.
Yous Spirit iz...
Yours.

She wills carry yous Home.
Member, what yous blood Mama told you? Jus for she die?
She bits dah backs of yous ears whens yous born.
So, only she knos yous. Yous neber be lost **no mo**.

She wills finds you.
She iz waiting fo you.
She is dreamin you.
She iz lookin to you.
She iz dancin fo you.
She iz ready fo you.

She iz singin yor name.

She iz singin yor name.

At Dah Promise Land.

Lonely Cravings

Lonely Crumbs
Endless inner space
Plays hide and seek
With shrinking shadows on the plate.

Survivors and Sacrifice
Of a hollow Unholy Hunger.
Imagination fills emptiness.
Anything fills emptiness.
Ravenous Rememberings.

Lonely Crumbs
Leaving. Lingering.
Lasting, Lamenting
Shadows of Nothingness.
Taste died days ago.
Tongue tied in solitary confinement.

Jealous Thoughts
Fight and Fail
Forgetting **far** away Flavors
And **far** away Feelings.

Slowly. Simple.
Scantily Seasoned Smells
Sick and slide inside
Memories of lingering

Lost lemon licks.

Mama said,
put a pebble
In your mouth
It keeps your tongue busy.

Acquainted aches.
Pitiful Pains become
Familiar Famished Friends.
Wanting Yesterdays
Become Tomorrows.

Chastised Crumbs
Chase each other
Around and around
On the plate.
Playing mind games.
Sounds become Smells.
Smells become Sounds.

Reality Voracious
Replacing Sadden Soulless Satisfaction.
Minus Morsels multiply in your mouth.

Survivors and Sacrifice
Of a Hollow Unholy Hunger.
Invisible Crumbs
In Exile
Exude into Eternity.

Long Languishing Stolid Shadows

Long Languishing
Stolid Shadows
Bruised by
Bittersweet Breeze.
Patiently Plays
Hide & Seek
With Autumns'
Lamenting
Lonely
Leaves.

Looking Forward Looking Backward

Looking Forward
Looking Backward
At the Same Time.

You Can Always Tell
You're at the Bissap Baobab,
Magical Mosaic Mbalax Music,
Mafe, Yassa, And A Side of
West African Hot Hip Hop
Your Heart Beats Faster
Than a Talking Drum
One Block Before 19th Street.

Complexity of Colors.
Liquidness of Languages.
Sounds. Tastes.
Sights of Senegal,
Hidden in the Mission.
Gather at the Little Baobab Tonight.

Close Your Eyes.
You are in Downtown Dakar.
Soft Ocean Breezes Dance
With the Taste of
Savory Seafood Coco.
Looking Forward
Looking Backward
At the Same Time.

Faces.
All Colors of the Human Rainbow.
Decked out In Fine Festival Ware.
Feels like Home
Under the Baobab Tree.

Everyone.
New and Old knows the Way.
Follow Me.
Dance, Drink, Dine
All At the Same Time.
One Common Thread
Holds this Tapestry Together...
Marco Senghor.
Loyal Friend.
Unforgettable Shy Smile.
Lives for His Family.
Today and Tomorrow.
Lover of Fairness and Justice.
Fighter for All People.
France, Senegal, San Francisco.
His Heart and Soul is Bissap Baobab.
Hc Welcomes the World...Home.
Everybody knows...Marco.

Greeted with...
Love Libations.
Infamous Ginger Juice
Totu, Fleur,
Tooni, Rose,
Sedem, Flamboyant

Flowing Faster than
His Friends Can Drink.
Homemade Love in a Glass.
Lively Conversation.
Bittersweet Beats on Fire.
Infectious Laughter.
Awaiting... Tender, Tasty,
Mouthwatering Gifts...
Pastelles.
Oh, Don't Forget
His World Famous Aloko.

Many, Many Travelers
Know the Soulful Sweet
Unforgettable Taste
Of Bissap Baobab's Aloko.
So Delicious. So Decadent.
Dreams Taste Good in Your Mouth.
Then One Day...
Along came Heartache and Happiness.
Marco knows Heartache and Happiness.
Wrapping around Him.
Knocking Him Down.
Kneeling at His Feet.
Kindness Almost Killed
Bissap Baobab.

But...
He Survived.
He Suffered.
He Succeeded.

A Broken Heart
Not A Broken Man.
Tragedy and Triumph.
Pain and Passion.
He Lost.
He Fought Hard.
He Won.
Always.
Looking forward.
Looking Backward.
At the Same Time.
An Amazingly Strong Wise Woman.
Raised her Only Sun.
She Knew.
He Was a Young King.

She Taught Him
Life and Death.
Her Love Lessons
Hidden in Secret Seeds
To Bloom Into
His Essence.
His Grit. His Gift.

To Always.
And Forever.

Be
A Proud.

African Man.

Looking Forward
Looking Backward

At the Same Time.

Mary Stallings Harlem Queen of the West

Mary Stallings

Velvet

Vivacious Voice.

Soothing. Soulful

Swooning.

Swinging

Sweet and Lovely.

Melting Mellow

Jazz Dewdrops.

Born

By

The City

By

The Bay.

Young Mary

Tenderly Touched

By Glorious Gospel.

Baby Steps and

Footprints from...

Laurel Heights

To Tokyo.

From The Black Hawk.

To Bangkok.

From The Monterey Jazz Festival

To Manila.

From The Hungry I

To I Have A Feeling.

Songs Were Made to Sing.

Mary Stallings.

She.

Sings like…

Soulful

Smoldering

<u>Slow</u>

Sax Solos.

Smoke burning embers

Whispering in the wind.

She sounds like.

Musical Smores

Melting in your ears.

Like Flowers and Flavors

In Freefall.

Fine and Mellow

In a Lazy **Dream**.

Lamenting

Lullaby of Leaves.

Violet Vibrations

Feelin' Good.

Her tones

You can taste

When you close your eyes and

Trust Your Heart

This Can't Be Love.

But Beautiful as you are

Your royal reign lives on and on

Remember Love.

And Love Remembers You.

Queen Harlem of the West

Mary Stallings.

Exquisite Elegance.

Graceful Goddess.

Majestic. Musical Melodies

Were Made For You.

Statuesque

Soul Siren

Shooting Stars

Envy her Light.

She Scats

Yesterdays Tomorrows.

Mellow Melting

Jazz Lullabies

Calmly Caress your spirit.

Flaming Hot Burning

But Beautiful

Down Home Blues.

Bebop Born Beaming

I Waited for You

On Divisadero Street.

Even Billie Holiday

Listens and Smiles.

Cats Like…

Count Basie

Wes Montgomery

Monk.

Earl Hines

Buddy Miles

Ben Webster.

Cal Tjader

Teddy Edwards.

And many,

Many more

Performed with you.

Don't Look Back

Look Forward.

I have a Feeling

The Future

Is Looking for You

Your jazz cannon

Is bursting at the seams.

Thank You Mary Stallings

Harlem of the West Queen

History Knows Your Name.

Mateen a Poem

"You get to decide
**What kind of King
You are going to be."**
Born with memory of Memories
Born to hold the past in your eyes
Born to love, lead, live, and look,
Born in a labyrinth of looking glasses legends
Vision sharpened with ancestral swords
Clear.
Deep.
Infinite.
Moonbeams dance with stardust
Shadows run with secret shy smiles.
"You are a good man
With a good heart."
**"You get to decide
What kind of King**
You are going to be."
African ashes birthmarks
Traces of the past futures
Knowledge embodied
Scars mark the way
To pass tomorrows.
"You are a good man
With a good heart."
**"You get to decide
What kind of King**

You are going to be."
Black Bold Beautiful
Blood lines
One drop
Bond us forever
One drop
Transcending
Time and Space.
One drop
Forever becomes today.
"You are a good man
With a good heart."
"Show them who you are."

Memories

I was born to live…forever.
To wander alone delicately
On cracked broken timeless lines.

I was born tangled with
Intangible
Invisible identities.
Baring bruised sorrows & stained-glass Secrets.

So. So, Tell me.
How do you measure
Fragments of feelings?

How do you measure
Fractions of Emotions?

Scattered. Severed
Puzzle Pieces of
When & Who & Where
& Never Never Why?

I was born to carry
Mountains & mountains of
Truth's Unwavering Commitments.

Born naked alone
In Between the lines of
A Single Solitary Sentence.

Born with two Birthmarks.
One invisible.

I was born to never die.
to Live in yesterday's moments
& Melancholy melodies.
To Live Fearless of Tomorrow's Fate.
To Live inside melanin muscle scars.
To Live with the tender touch
Of tragic traumas.

To Live inside the shadows of Dreams.
Inside the Shadows of Fears.
& Inside the Shadows of Jaded Joy.

Born to Live Frozen.
Silent from every unspoken language.
Born To live Adjacent
To drum beats & heartbeats.

I was born the day before
Rainbows chose their colors.

You'll find me
On blank pages
Of every unsolved mystery.
Found buried
In tombs of the unborn.

I was born before the Beginning

Knew the Final Ending.
I was born to never change. Never die.
Born to Heal, Born to Hurt,
Born to Help, Born to Hope.

Flames Burn with Envy
In Awe of
My Taste. My Tones. My Touch. My Tears.
As they whisper stolen Tales of the Dead.

I was Born with
Lonely Lasting Lyrics & Poems
Silently Stitched inside of Mama's Quilts.
Desperately Decoding Destiny Dreams.

Born to Eternally Echo Echo Echo
Songs Ancestral Sirens forgot.
My Childhood Never became My Adulthood.

Because…
I was born of Broken Promises
& White Lazy Lingering Little Lies.

I was born to Wait & Watch & Wonder.
Born to Question. To Ponder.
Born to Grieve & Crave Unknown Endings.
So…?
When will Premature Shadows
Awaken from Darkness?
From chasing hidden shards of blinding light?

When will I see and feel?
Flawless Fertile Freedom?
Walking around with seeds in her pockets?

When will I know
Her soft touch. Her velvet suede skin?
Unbought. Unbossed.
Unlocked, Unshackled from her past.

So. So, You Tell me,
Tell me.
Do you know
When
Missing Melaninated Memories Stop Masquerading
And Become History?

Miss Mary Ellen Pleasant

Miss Mary Ellen Pleasant

Your Fiery Passion
Defied Danger & Death.
You Plant Herbs of Your Ancestors.
You Sing Coded Secret Songs
To the Enslaved.

Your Beauty Crossed Color Lines.

Your Ingenious Ingenuity
Alerted Passengers
On The Underground Railroad.

Your Birthmarks
DNA Gifts
From Your
Vodou Queen Grandmother.
Madame Marie La Veau.
She Knew. She Knew.

She Knew.
Your Black Intelligentsia.
Your Wealth. Your Courage.
Your Dignity. Your Generosity. Your Grace.

Your **Black
Life
Mattered**.

To More than
Just a Few.

Your Wild & Wondrous
Warrior Goddess
Accomplishments
Enshrined in Museums.

Your Disbelieving Deeds Defined
Delicate Destinies.

Your Life Paths
Intersectional & Multi-Dimensional.

You Walked & Crawled.
You Strolled & Sprinted.

You Danced the Jig
On Bloodied - Black Feet.
During 1817-1904.

Your Herstory
Hidden In the Columns
Of History.

Your Fragile Fragments
Linger on Streets

Bush & Octavia,
Old Town San Francisco.

Full moon Mornings
Your Ghostly Mist
Floats Free
Down Foggy
Fillmore Hills.

Your Over Dressed Spirit
Cake Walks Down
Paths of Social Justice.

Cake Walks Down
Paths of Kindness & Deceit.

Cake Walks Down
Paths Littered
With Sharp Shards
From Ceramic & Crystal Ceilings
You Cracked & Shattered.

Leaving Bloodied Fingers
From The First Black Feminist
Millionaire.

Miss Mary Ellen Pleasant.

Cake Walks Down
Paths of Patriarchal Democracy.

Slowly Strolling
Down Paths of Power.
Painted with Periwinkle Passion.

Miss Mary Ellen Pleasant.

Born Enslaved. Born to Survive.
Born to Run Businesses & Guns.

Born to Finance Abolitionists.
Born To Spy on Confederate Generals.

Born Female.
Born to Manipulate
Men & Their Senseless Systems.

Born to Grow Old
In Sonoma County.

Born to Excel & Exceed
Thirty Million$
One Lifetime.

Your French Perfume
Mildly Mephitic
Of Espionage & Lavender
On Silk Gloves.

Miss Mary.

You were On Fire.
Burning.

Sexism & Ageism.
Racism & Feminism.
Classism & "Maryism."

What A Time It Was!

White Men
Haunted You
Down in Hate.

White Men
Fearlessly
Fell in Love
At Your Feat.

White Men
Sued You
In Calloused Courts.

White Men
Courted You
in Parlors with Port.

Yes.
Rest.
Rest in Power.
Rest in Gratitude.
Rest in Respect.

Rest.
Your Full Life.

Your Memories.
Your Dreams.
Your Herstories.

All Rest.
With You
In Sonoma County.

Thank You.
Miss Mary Ellen Pleasant.

Mother of Human Rights in California.

Mothers' Love

Many days and many nights

Only you were

There to comfort me and

Hug me with warm whispering wings.

Ending all fears.

Releasing all doubts.

Sun Beams and Mom Beams

Lovingly last forever.

Outstands your

Virtue and Love for all

Eternity.

My Father

A
Simple.
Single.
Shadowed.
Shaded
Photo.
Black, White, Grey.
Wrinkled.
Worn.
Weary Like Winter.
Standing Center Framed
Bare Chest Brave
A Tall Lean "Drink of Water"
In Dusty Dry Faded Fatigues
A Black & Proud
World War II U.S. Army Soldier

Planted in Pounding,
Passionate Morning Sunlight
On Some Forgotten Beach...
Alone.
Before I was born.
A Single Photo. A Single Clue.
Priceless.
Lifelong Mystery.
My Father.
A Ghost? A Secret?
A Myth? A Mist of Truth?

His Name Never
In Anyone's Mouth.
He was Invisible.
He was Incomparable. He was elusive.
Until…March 2021.
I found Him. Waiting to be Found.
Tangled in the Middle of the
World Wide Web.
You Can Find Anything
On the Internet. It's true.
That Rabbit Hole of
DNA Lives Forever and Ever.

John Buster Pickett.
My Father. Is Real.
He Became.
My Velveteen Rabbit.
He Became. "Real."
You See. "To Become "Real."
It takes a long time.
That's why it doesn't happen to people who
Break easily. Or who have
To be carefully kept.
Generally, by the time you are Real,
Most of your hair has been loved off,
And your eyes drop out
And you get loose in the joints
And very shabby.
But those things don't matter at all,
Because once you are Real

You can't be ugly,
Except to people who don't understand."

I Understand.
I Understand *who* You Are.
I Understand *what* You Are.
I Understand *why* You Are.
I Understand *where* You Are.
I Understand *now* You Are.
I Understand.
I Understand Why
Fingers Tingle When Numb.
Feels like Old Knowledge Made New.

I See You. I See Me.
I See John Buster Pickett.
You are Real.
You are My Father.
I Love You.
I Always Will.

My North Star

Miles and miles of melanin midnight sky
Yesterdays' nights daydream about her.
Queen of the Mid-Morning Star.
Nine nights. Ninety-nine million steps nearer to North
And her Naked Negro Shade.

Orion's nighttime lover.
Lonely. Lamentingly longs for Freedom.
Remembering their secrets…
Remembering their resilience…
Remembering…
Ten Thousand whispers
Each effortlessly echoing
Frederick Douglass's wise whispering words
Wet with the Blood ink of Liberation.

They fly below the storm.
Ten Thousand side-eye slants
Saw Harriet secretly slip silently.
Quilts on trees. Quilts on fences.
Sing silently to the North Star.
Hundreds of hidden less words hiding in plain sight
See through history's carefully cataract careless eyes.

Sunday's sunset slides in after supper
Hiding crystal cache clouds in their eyes.
Time. Time.
Time to Travel.

Down Deep
On the Underground Road of Rails

One Way along the North Star's Cosmic Tracks
"You don't need no ticket; you just get on board."
Ancestral footprints fill your shoes with love and night
visions.

Remembering. Remembering.
Real Human Heroes
Dead & Alive.
So steal "A" way.
Steal Away.
Steal any way.
Anyway
Home.

Nia

Nia.
Purpose.
Her seeds were planted
On this day.
And On this day
We sow those seeds
Watered with
Confirmed clarity of conviction,
Renewing your Purpose.
Nia.

Children often say,
"I didn't do it "on purpose."
"I didn't mean to do it."
"It's not my fault."

Remember those days?
You and I have said those same
Words many, many times.
First, we get "caught."
Then, we speak our "truth.

How did we learn to **spin** our truth?
How did we learn
Not to be accountable?

Why Are we **so** Afraid
To face consequences?

Why Are we **so** Afraid
To pay that
Unknown debt called
Accountability?

Walk down that lane of memory.
Listen to the words along the way.

"OOO, You gonna get in trouble."

Remember those words?
Those words would freeze you with Fear.

Those words
hit you in
The **back** of your head.
A sharp slap of reality

Asking
Those Ageless Queries.

What is
The true cost of Truth?

What is the
Cost of being accountable?

Do we know
what it means
to forgive ourselves?

Do we know
how to be
Intimate with
Truth?

Do we know what it means
to have
"Clean consequences?"
Nia knows.

Nia.
Her seeds are
Permanently planted
On this day.
On this day
Renewing our purpose.
Know Nia.

So, how do we teach
Nia
To ourselves
and
To our children?

Start with **truth.**

Ask yourself which truth is true?

The stories of our ancestors Birthed our **truth**.
But they are not just stories.

They are DreamMaps;
Filled with Seeds,
Blueprints, Hidden Messages,
Brainstorms, Secrets, Trust, Songs, Poems, Solutions, Proverbs,
Wizdom, Potions, Lullabies, Libations,
Intuitions, Recipes, Daydreams, Spirit,
Shea Butter,
Mother Wit, Prayers, Intentions, Mysteries, Puzzles,
Music,
and so much more.

It's Our Love Language
Of African Intelligentsia.
Filled with
Secret codes
Waiting with Wizdom Wishes.

Connecting dots to our **truth.**
Connecting to our Purpose.

We all know well
Our "Lamenting Legacy of Consequences".
We Live inside

Long, Long, Lamenting Legacy of Consequences.
Our
Historic Horrors Hibernate
Deep in our DNA.
Our
Stormy Stories of Struggle and Survival.

Middle Passage, Slavery, Jim Crow, Revolution, Prison
Industrial Complex, Oppression, Rebellion,
Resilience, Lynching, Revolts, Defiance, Freedom.

Our
Ancient Afro Futures.

We know it like the "black" of our hands.
Take a Long Look…
In the mysterious mirror of memory.
Find…your stories.
Your history. Your herstory.

Find Your Nia.
Your Purpose.

Her seeds are planted
On this day.
On this day
We sow those seeds and
Renew our purpose.
Nia.

So, Sit and Listen
at the feet of our Elders,

Look deeper in the cracks of mirrors,
Seek the Shadows of Spirit,
Gaze Deep within Daydreams,
Trust their Echoes,

Their Voices, their Visions,
Whispering in your Ears.
Dancing in your Morning Dreams.

Question.
Constantly Critically think
What it really means
To stand up for your convictions?
Or Not.

It's Your African
Ancestral Royal Legacy.
Yours to carry on & sustain
Your African Ancestral Royal Legacy.
AKA
Kwanzaa.
The principles of the First Fruits.
7 days
To discover, explore, expand your knowledge.
Kwanzaa is our Black "ONLY" fountain
When thirsty.
Drink in
Clean Cool Clear
Waters of Knowledge.
Know
Who you are.
Where you came from.
Where You are going.

Ask the Ancestors.

They know.

Accept accountability of
Your Ancestral African Legacy?

Trust your Ancestors
Trust their timeless,

Endless, countless stories.
Rarely read in books.

Until Kwanzaa.
These principles tell us

To Take **Time** to Think.

To **Take Time to Explore** your Legacy.

To Take Time to Find your Purpose.

To Take Time to Discover Nia.

Your Ancestors stories
Are filled with purpose.
Posturing with Power, Pride, Passion and Purity.

Stories **Tell** Us.
Stories **Teach** Us,
Stories **Teleport** Us,
Stories **Sankofa** Us,

To The Past.
To Understand the Present.
To Prepare for the Future.

Cruise Ship "Sacred Sankofa awaits."

An old Mponque African proverb says,
"Do not throw away the oars
Before the boat reaches the shore."
Keep your oars,
Keep them close.
You never know
When you might need them.

Remember your ancestors are always listening.

Nia.
Purpose.
Her seeds of purpose are planted
On this day.
And On this day
We sow those seeds and
Renew your purpose.

Nia.
Wonders…
What kind of ancestor are you going to be?

Ode to Mr. T

Ode to Mr. T.
His First Thoughts
Race Too Quickly.
They Chase Themselves
Into a Warm Welcoming
Glimpse. Glimmering...
Remembering... Reflecting...

Good Thoughts.
Good Feelings.
Good Words.
Good People.
Good Food.
Good Brew.

GoodEarth, Wind & Fire.
Good Water. Good Music.
Good Life. Good Love.
All At the Same Time.
His Shy Smile.
His Unconditional Laugh.
Covers Him Like a
Warm Wakandian Blanket.
His Thoughts
In the Morning May Breeze
Soon Blow Away with
"being too happy with thine happiness."

His Tender Bass Voice
Carries Cheeky Tunes
Twisted with a Hint of Humor
Makes Your Heart Hum
In Three Part Harmony.

His Favorite Far Away
Melody From a Time
Long, Long Ago.
In A Galaxy, Far, Far Away.
You Can "See" His Muse
Deep Inside Him.
His Clever Sense
His "Laughter Charms"
Hidden in His Secret Language for Life.
His Goodhearted Guide
"Music" Gently
Navigates His Path.
Uncertain at First
Charted Well in Memory.
Echoes Far, faraway "Freedom"
A Richie Havens Song.
He Quenches His Thirst
With WildnWet
Double Dry Martinis
Ice Cold Local Malt Beer
In A Tall Frosty
Equally Iced-Cold Glass.

Colder Than Early Morning
Camping Chills.

Until...
The Water Maven
Awakened with Siren Calls
To Swim and Swim and Swim.
Dolphins and Mermaids.
Dolphins and Mermaids.
Sun Kissed Sands Against Splashing Sea Surf.
The World Knows
His Footprints.
His Lightfoot
Treads Heavy

With a Hearty Healthy Heavenly Taste

For... Simply,
The Best.
Burnt. Bigheaded.
Barefaced. Blissful.
Butt Kicking.
BBQ.
Roasted & Rooted.
In Austin & Dallas Texas.
His Place Always Set at The Table.
No Stranger to His Tastebuds.
Familiar Flavors Follow Him Home.
Hot Sauce, Hot Dogs, Kosher Dills, and Homemade Brisket.

His Neck Neatly Adorned
With Golden Links.
Each Link. A Trip Around the Sun.
Each Link. A Classroom Treasure.

For Being...
A Scholar with a Green Thumb.
A Traveler. An Explorer.
A Teacher. A Partner.
A Friend.
Who Loves Life.
And Life Loves...

Mr. T.

One

This poem **"One"** was written in honor of the **100**th Birthday of the home **351** Santa Clara Avenue, Oakland, CA.

One
The most magical number next to zero.
It shapes Everything,
And all things Effortlessly.
Playful. It hides and seeks.
Now you see it.
Now you don't.

You find yourself thinking,
Pondering what is real?
Ask Alice.
Ask the Velveteen Rabbit.
She knows.

Today, we discover that **one**
Solitary silent "**one**" has moved
99 times.
Gracing us with a
Celebratory Century of baby steps.

Each baby step opens
100 infinite illusive
Indelible
Delicate Dreams
That found their way home,

Here at 351 Santa Clara Avenue
Their moments prematurely frozen
Only to melt away the past
In some distant future.

Yes, we all want to know
What the walls heard, saw and felt.
Timeless moments frozen faceless forever.
Sixteen Savory secrets,
Left-handed lost and lonely lies,
Sweetened from ripened fruit of
Regretful imaginations and daydreams.
They secretly smile knowing
With or without us.
That this day would become real…or is it?

100…99…98…97
You lullaby yourself
Into a place of childlike calm and carelessness.
Listening in-between your spaces of silence.
Hear the Love.
Here is Love.
Hear the Hope.
Here is Hope.
Hear the Pain of the past.
It will carry you **one** step.
To the next step.
To **one** hundred and **one** steps.
Never reaching the beginning…
Or the end…

Once Upon a Masterpiece
a poem for Duke and Billy

One Frosty Full Moon December Night
Not that Long Ago
A Musical
Daring Double Dream
Dosing and Drifting
Dosing and Drifting
Into the Masterminds' Ears
Of The VIP's of Jazz.

World Famous Jazz's Dynamic Duo.
D. & B.
Mr. Edward Kennedy Ellington &
Mr. William Thomas Strayhorn.
AKA. Duke and Billy.

Duke said,
"Billy,
Your Brainwaves are **in** my head,
And mine are **in** yours."

Billy said, "Duke and I
Changed the <u>mood</u> a bit.

All the themes are there,
But they're wearing
Different threads- you dig."

They Touched the Tender Tones of Tchaikovsky.

They Tasted Cornbread and Gingerbread.

They Transformed the Old World Classic

Into the Harlem Renaissance in **1960.**

THE NUTCRACKER SUITE WAS TRANSFORMED.

Billy took the lead to Crack open **this** Nut.

Their Dreamy Negro Night Visions

Came Complete with

A Script, A Score.

A Cast of Dancers and Musicians.

All in Living Color.

The Star.
A Wise and Wonderful
Wooden Nutcracker.
Not like any Cracker of Nuts.
This Magic Nutcracker was Transformed.

And just like
The Velveteen Rabbit.
He Became Real.

Do you know
The Old Secret Recipe?
How to Become Real?

First, You Need…
Five Fresh Fairy Wing Wishes.

One Cup Winter Warm Coco
Made from the darkest Senegalese Chocolate
You can find.

Topped with a Double Dollop of Caramel Cream.

Made from Magic Moroccan **Marshmallows.**

Sprinkle Jamaican Ginger.

Gently pour Thirty-three Cups
Hot. Juicy. Jazz Drops.

Now. Mix. Stir.
Sauté. **Simmer.**
Fry. Bake.
Then Broil in your favorite
Gumbo pot on an open fire.

Carefully, Add
One Daring Dash of
Scotch Bonnet
Pepper Flakes.

Sip slowly
On a Frosty Full Moon Night
In December.
And **That's** how.
You Become Real.

A Mysterious Old Magician's Magic
Begins the Dreamers' Catalyst.

One Tiny, Tiny, Trick
Leads you far, far.

Into this Furious
Fantastic Fantasy Adventure.
Filled with
First Positions.
Graceful Gliding Glissades.
Swingin Beats.
Mice Kings / Queens.

Soldiers Battling.
Jumping Jazz Joints.

Children Laughing.

Flavors Dancing.

Drink **in** the Dream
At **Drossy Place.**
Sip **S l o w l y.**
AHHHHH. Swallow Smooth.

Smell the Aromas of
Tasty Teas Tangoing with your tongue.

Caressing Coffees
Strong enough to walk home.

Embrace Creamy Hot Chocolates
Reminiscent of Childhood Yesteryears.

And Don't Forget
The Best of the Best.
Chilly Cherry Rum.
One shot, I mean just one shot is all you need,
and you really know
The True Meaning of **Fa La La.**

Melting Musical Movements
Mesmerized you.

Tunes like
"Toot Toot Tootie Toot."

Sounds like

Clever Calliope.
Pumping out tunes again
On Coney Island Pier.

Soul Train Strut downtown
Following footsteps to
Gin Ling Way
In Chinatown.

Where **All** Roads Lead
To the Coolest Club in Harlem.
Drossy Place.

Pirouettes, Prancing and Dancing
On Polished Pristine Parkade floors.

Cats Blowing Hot and Heavy
Jamming Jazz Joints
All night lon**g**.
Till the break of dawn.

Duke once said,
"Billy, "Your brush with the classics is genius."

We've got Tchaikovsky.
Tapping his toes.

Dancing with the "Flore adores."
Now, your tongue
tickles

With the
Taste of Turmeric
Of that freshly baked
"Arabesque Cookie."
Hmmmm. Hmmmm, Good.

Duke Ellington and Billy Strayhorn

"Deeply valued the musical personalities.

Of **Each** of their Band Members.

They **Always** kept in mind a
Player's **unique** sound

Whenever composing music.

Thank you, Duke Ellington.

Thank you, Billy Strayhorn.

The VIP's of J. A. Z. Z.

Your Genius Compositions
Have changed the world forever.

We love you madly

Open Your Eyes

Open Your Eyes
Listen Loudly.

Let light pour!
Magical notes
Slowly finding
Hints and Echoes.

Sounds Silently Seduce
Harmonizes. Hums.

Note by Note
Drop by Drop.

Notice
Colors Serenade.

Watch
Light Ride and Slide.

Mathematical
Multi-Rhythms.

Tornado Into
Giant Gingerly Gales

Gently Kissing Your Cheek
Wet With

Wild is the Wind.

Effortless Esperanza
Carefully Caresses

Future Fantasies
Infinite Imaginations.

Eyes clearly hear.
When watching

Wayne Shorter's
Daily **Weather Report.**

So, Open
Your ThirdEye.

Jump off.

All Auditory Cliffs
And
Look
Up.

Feel
Soft Baby Breezes
Cake Walk.
Herbie Hancock's
Watermelon Man

Sauntering and Strolling
Into your mind's eye.

See Silent Crystals
Sparkle. Shine.

On Bill Evans keys.

Experience, Explore, Examine Jazz
With your eyes
Wide Open.

Listen Covertly.

Shapes. Contours.

Sounds Sing
Loud with Melodic Melanin.

Now you See.
How fully Alive

You Are

Watching. Wondering.
Why
Lines Blur in Silence.

Seeing with your Ears

Some say a Superpower.

I say.

"Open your eyes **wide.**
Watch and Wonder.
Why
Jazz plays
Hide and Seek
With your Inner Vision."

Smile.
Virtual Video Games
Silently. Suddenly
Surround You.

Jazz's Soundtrack.
Intersects
Your Cyber Cerebral Cortex.

Robert Glasper
Stuck in your head.

Befitting a
Black **Superhero.**
Standing
Right in Front of You.

Jazz Sees.
See Jazz.

Listen with your eyes.

Melodic melodies
Make Magic!

Now you see it.
Now you don't.

Now you hear it.
Now you won't.

JazzPaints
Neon colors

Improvising.

3D and 5G and Dolby 7.3

Visual soundtracks
Blow Minds with

Ultra-Supersonic Symbols
Called **Now.**

Rhythms
Slide and Slow

InTo Silence and Surprise.

Ride Hard.

Hold on tight.

Billy Higgins **Impressions**

Tastes like Ghost Peppers
On your tongue.

Eyes water.
Knowing why
Tears taste like salt.

See Jazz.
Jazz Sees.

Jazz
+ and -
X and divides
=ing…

Hues and shadows.
Bass and Tenor.
Harmony and Discord.
Sunlight and Midnight.

So,
Visually
Be
Jazz.

HearJazz,

When Whispering
Wes Montgomery's

Bumpin' on Sunset

Lingering **inside** your gaze
Tasting Butterscotch sundaes
In your ear.

Imagine
Two friends
Meet
On Bourbon Street.

Audio and Visual.

They Love.
They Create.
They Jam
They Jest Joviality
Simultaneously.

Daringly **Drive.**
Co-conspirator / Copilot.
Jazz Junior.

Traffic Transforms, and
Slowly Electric Slides
In Unison.

When Chick Corea
Takes the Wheel.

Walk a million Miles
He'll show you

All his Blues.
And So Much More.

So,
Wake up
Imagine.
Auditory.
Intelligentsia
Visually.

See with your **Ears.**
Hear with your **Eyes.**

See Jazz.
Jazz Sees.

What do
You see
When
You see
Jazz?

Overwhelming

Overwhelming.
Overflowing.
Inundating.

Neverending.

Enduring.
Effortless.
Reckless.

Love of God.

Grace Gingerly Guides.
Spirit Silently Sings.

Warming your heart
To open.

To Be Free.

To See.
God.

Beginnings without
Endings.

Constant Calm Caresses.

Healing. Healing. Healing.

Faultless Faith.
Feverishly Finds you.

Opening Hardened Hearts.
Baby Steps Become Believing.

Trusting Tender
Timeless Transformation.

You See God.
God Sees You.

Deferring Devotion
Delicately Damaged with Doubt.

Eternally Erased with Endless
Angelic Ashes of Absolution.

Plethora of Pious Praises.
Pure Perfection.

God Knows.
Know God.

First Forgiveness
Finally Freedom Forever.

Overwhelming.

Overflowing.
Inundating.

Neverending.

Enduring.

Effortless.

Reckless.
Love
of God.

God Sees.
See God.

God Hears.
Hear God.

God Knows.
Know God.

God Loves
Love God.

Peggy's Poem

Bon Voyage!!! Congratulations!!!

You.
Are about to Embark upon
Your Most Prodigious
Astounding Adventure
Into Life's Metamorphosis.
AKA Retirement.

For such an Occasion,
A Magic Muse
Has Gifts to Bestow.
She.
Is now your Mentor.
Bound with Messages
That will
Make You Mill and Murmur
At Any Given Moment
Midnight or Morning.

Messages Magically Multiply
Into A Mild Militant,
Yet, Mindful Mosaics of
Malingering Motivations.

She.
Brings Full Moonless Mornings

That Melt into a Mirage of Dreams,
Dreams, and More Dreams.

She.
Will
Meticulously

Mirror and Mock
Mazes of Forgotten
Missed Opportunities
While Wishing
Them Farewell.

Mischievous
is She.
A Metamorphic Mist. Ready.
At the Wink of an Eye
To Magically
Lose your Cell Phones,
Tablets, iPads, Laptops,
And Keys of any kind.

Replaced with Siren-like Moments
That Mesmerize
Defy All Meaning
And Time.

This Misfit Mentor is yours Peggy.

To mass ALL your
Mind-boggling

Milestones & Memories,
Insightful Inspirations.

Those Euphoric "Ah Ha" Moments.
That will be the
SEEDS and Maps
All Your Students
Treasure.
As their Destinies Forever.
Thank you. Peggy
This poem is dedicated to my friend.

Poem for Barbara

Another word
For Sister
Is Friend.

My SisterFriend
My Sister Barbara.
We get our childhoods again.
Hearts humming harmonize
Lost and Found at the same time.

Sisters Sing your name
Sisters Dance til dawn
Sisters Daydreams
Become Sweet Realities.

My
Sister.
Old becomes new.

My
Family.
Past becomes future.

Friendship
So powerful...
Mountains get jealous.
Clouds fades without shadows.
Rainbows know

Their Colors will
Always be there.

My
SisterFriend.
Bonded beyond
Time.
Bonded beyond
Now and Yesterday.

Strong.
Sassy.
Steadfast.
Soulful.
Stamina.
Shadows of struggles throw shade.

Show them who you are.
Black Blood Diamond.
Shine. Sing. Shout.

Sisters Sing your name
Sisters Dance til dawn
Sisters Daydreams
Become Sweet Realities.

My
Family.

My
Friend.

My
Sister

Is Love

Pop Quiz Number 1

Ready?
Where are
the
Stewards of Humanity?

Where are
the Revolutionaries?

Where are
Their BFF's?

Have you seen
The Change Agents?

Have you seen
The Peacekeepers lately?

Where are the Real Ones
We've been
Waiting for?

Are they coming?
Are they coming soon?

Their Shadows were
Last seen

Playing
Hide & Seek
Dodging
Death. Disaster.
And Decisions.

Did they **slide** in your DM's?
Or did they RSVP?

What did they tell you?
What did they dream?

Are they suffering?
Are they safe?

What were their last words?
Did they speak For or Against?

Did they graffiti Walls of Victory
Or Walls of Violence?

Did their Nightmares & Daymares
Finally face each other?

Whose reflections are
Buried in the cracks of mirrors?

Will they Remember
The Daydreams
of

The Dead?

Will they Remember
Stolen Names
Forgotten
In Tomorrows'
Lost & Found?

Are there any
Safe Zones
Left?

Or just
Silent
Safe Words?

Listen.
Can you hear them?
Can you hear
Their words
Echoing off Cliffs
Of Despair?

How old are those
Ageless Egalitarian Agreements?

Who will
Be

The Last **One**
Standing?

Will you
Stand
with them?

Will you
Stand
With me?

Where do you
Go
When Streets are
Full
Of Empty Lies
Of
Quiet Genocide?

Where do children
Play
Without guns?

Whose songs
will Haunt
You

And Haunt you
And Haunt you

With barren beats
For eternity?

Is Love Real?

<u>Who</u>
Are
The Stewards
of Humanity?
<u>Who</u>
Are
The Revolutionaries?

Will Blood
Be
The New Water?

Will the Change Agents
Finally, finally,
arrive
On time?
Or
After, After
The Peacekeepers?

RAGE
A Circle Poem

In an Empty Ebony Eternity
Rakishly Repulsing **RAGE**
Traumatizes Twisted Tirades
With Wicket Wreck less Word Wars.

Dovetailing Cognitive Defiant Dissonance
On Withering Windless Wafts.
Bilking Explosive
Emaciated Emancipated Egos.

Bloodlessly Bleeding Boggs & Boggs & Boggs
Of Decayed Defiled **Dread.**

Catastrophically Cursed
With Endless Ethereal Extremities
Of Broken Promises
Perniciously Propagating
In An Empty Ebony Eternity.

Rakishly Repulsing **RAGE**
Traumatizes Twisted Tirades.
With Wicket Wreck less Word Wars.

Dovetailing Cognitive Defiant Dissonance
On Withering Windless Wafts.
Bilking Explosive

Emaciated Emancipated Egos.

Bloodlessly Bleeding Boggs & Boggs & Boggs
Of Decayed Defiled **Dread.**

Catastrophically Cursed
With Endless Ethereal Extremities
Of Broken Promises
Perniciously Propagating
In An Empty Ebony Eternity.
RAGE.

Remember

Comfortless Creaking.
Clear.
So clear.
Concave Crackling.
Broken Crystal chards
Clandestinely chilled.
They Hide and Seek
Secretly
        Seducing
            Silence.
Calmly common.
Creepy at first.
Rhythmic.
Relentless. Light House
Searching Siren Solos
Endlessly echoing
Sheer
Slight
Newborn Whispers
Enchanting
Enshrouding
Savory Sunless Shadows
Emanating
Entombing
Your Endless Eclipse.
Simultaneously.
Sharpening
Seven Soulful Senses.

Fearlessly
Free falling
Into
    in through
               Inside
Our Outer Space.
Wrestling
        Wrinkled
                  wordless
Windswept memories.
Each
Exquisitely
Escapes
Inception.
Four
        Familiar
                  formless
Delicate Dreams
Disguised as
Dainty defiant
Ravenous
        Rabbit
                Holes
Wildly whimpering
Wet
Warm Wisdom.
Your Sixth & Seventh Sense
Burns bitter with
Indigo
Icy

Inbred
Intuition.

DeJa' Vu
Slow Dancing
Dangerously
With
Reality…
Again

Remember Part Two

I Remember
The Days of Rain.
The First Night.
Long.
Lingering.
Lamenting.
For Bittersweet Seasons.
Winter.
Summer.
Spring.
Fall.
Strutting down a Cloudy Cat Walk
Next to a Carousel.

Now Imagine a Race.
A Rainbow Race.
To The Finish Line.
The Greens Run the Fastest.
Leaving No Shadows.
They Cross First.

Last…
Labyrinth Lagging.
The Blues.
Lonely.
Lost.
Late.
Lazy.

Laborious Blues.

Chilled by Midnight's
FullMoon Memories of
Fragile Forest Fires
Fondly Flaming Forever.

Leaving.
Lost.
Lethargic.

Remembering

I remember.
I remember.
I remember the first days a rain/reign.
The first nights of stars at dust.
99 long lingering lightless nights
Yet, lightning quick after a blink.
Lonely. Lamenting for a lost
Bittersweet Savory Flowerless Season
called Spring.
Catching after Summer's Autumn.
Waiting why Winter is late.
Imagine the Four Seasons
Together, stuttering down some Cloudy Catwalk.
Imagine the Rainbows Racing
To the finish line.
The Greens run the fastest.
Leaving no shadows,
Just quiet puffs of dust.
They cross first into
A lavender labyrinth.
Lagging last, you'll find the Blues.
Longing. Lost. Late.
You know they're always late
Wondering will I ever cross
That endless finish line?

Samba

Samba.
Soft. Smooth.
Caramel Samba.
Rhapsody of Rhythms
Slow dance with your Soul

Suddenly skips...a beat
As it slowly quickens
Samba
Sensually senses Siren Calls
Heart Beat. Heart Beat. Heart Beat. Heart Beat.
Awakened Senses...Smile
As They All Crowd the Dance Floor
To Celebrate...Jobim, Getz, Mendes, Gilberto, Djavan, and
Gato.

Samba. Samba.Samba.
Your African Grandmother
Whispers silent soothing lullabies.
She sends warm, whimsical shockwaves.
Leaving Slender
Summer Breezes jealous.

Serene Sunrises.
Swollen Sunsets.
Drums in discourse scream
Ginga. Ginga. Ginga. Ginga.

Carnival. Carnival. Carnival.
Dance. Dance. Dance. Dance. Samba. Samba. Samba.

You
Slowly Slide
Your wet toes sculpting
Clandestine Messages
On the Tall and Tan and Lovely
Silky skin of Rio Beaches.

Where Filho Worships You.
Moonlight shadows
You with Star Dust.
Sun Kissed Waves
Caress and capture...You
Samba. Samba. Samba.

You Swing. You Sweat.
You Sway. You Swoon.

You Know.
You Feel.
You Smile.
You hum...
So Sweetly
All your secret lovers
Blush
At the same time.

Oh, This Music.
This Samba.

This palate of Magical Flavors
Spicy...Savory
Saucy...Sweet
Always HOT.
Samba. Samba. Samba.

Bittersweet
Passions ignite.
Implode. Never-ending.
Nexus. Natures' Naughty and Nice.
Samba. Samba. Samba.
You go on...
And on...And on...And on...
Till the Break of Dawn.

Sea Tears

The only planet with oceans and seas.
Oceans and seas that cover more than land.
Oceans and seas form a single body of water.
Oceans and seas with mountains taller
Then Mt. Everest & as deep as the Grand Canyon.
Silently sleep beneath the waves.

Currents surround the globe with wind and weather.
Touching the water will warm your fingers or freeze them.
This Liquid majesty holds ice bergs & tropical islands.
Who reigns over this royal water wonderland?

King Neptune.
He rules the Oceans & Seas.
He invites you to close your eyes.
Listen.
As he exhales, waves are released…free
As he inhales, tides are pulled and pushed
From the light of the moon.

His whispers awaken Sleeper Waves
Slowly growing
Imploding & Exploding
On the stormy shores.
He washes the sand
Incessantly.
Until each golden grain

Is crystal clean.
Becoming a shining diamond shell of the sea.

Millions of abandoned waves
Creep and crawl
From the bottomless Black Floors
To the Sun Filled beaches.
Chasing and Dancing
In Between Time & Wind.
Caught in a Circular current
Endlessly turning and returning.

Ancestor Waves chase their children
Never knowing their names.
Grandfather Tides crash and linger
Leaving baby bubbles
Rippling, Trickling Trails of Sea Tears.

Tears become waves.
Waves become tides.
Tides tenderly touch
The Night Sky sending
Mesmerizing Milky way Moonbeams
Making magical music for a
Never ending Dance.
Sirens only sing about.

Sea Tears
Waiting, Wishing, Wanting
To become Watery Dreams.

That silently sleep
Deep. Deep inside seashells.

King Neptune Knows.
The rocking rhythm
Soul of the sea.
The Pulse.
The Heartbeat.
It all Begins at the bottomless floor
Inside the hollow heart
Of the first Mermaid.
Yemoja.

Seasons Around the Sun
A Birthday poem for Anissa

Nineteen Hundred SeventyThree
Pink Floyd gave us Money.
Gladys and the Pips gave us
Midnight Train to Georgia.

Joe Burnley and Margaret Carpenter
Gave us you. Anissa.

Born first and last in so many ways.
You were the captain of your own Pirate ship.
Navigating International Seas & Russian
Rivers.
Navigating Lauren, Keleigh, Kia, and Kenzie
too.
Commanding playgrounds
To swimming pools.
Sky diving and hot air balloons.
Angelic Voice like a siren in disguise.
With a Wild Wise Brain bursting inside.

You boarded your midnight train...Early
Traveling: Cross country USA,
UK, Europe, Egypt, Caribbean,
Mexico, South Africa, Australia,
Greece, Cuba, Japan, Russia,
and don't forget Disneyland.

Twelve trips around the Sun.
Singing at the United Nations.
And so much more...

There are infinite words.
There are infinite colors.
And there are infinite gifts.

Word Smiths, Painters and Poets.
All Gather to celebrate you today.
Your favorite day of the year.
The day you were born.
For this auspicious occasion
The Four Seasons
Warmly, wisely welcomed you.

Winter, Spring, Summer and Fall.
They stood tall
Holding you, Loving you.
From that first minute
After midnight
October first ages ago.
Crisp, chilled air
kissed
By frozen blue skies.
Full Moon shadows
Even made the stars blush.

Their presence commemorates
This special, historic day.
Winter, Spring, Summer and Fall.

AKA.
Winter-Sophia
Spring-Giavanna
Summer-Natalia
Fall-Graham
Each shaping and sprinkling your seasons
With Words, Gifts and Colors.

And most of all Love.

"Winter-Sophia
(Sophia reads below)

"I give you one single word
For your birthday.
That word is Sweet.

When I think of you,
All I can think of is
"Sweet"

Because you created me.
And I exist because of you.
You gave me **life.**
That was pretty **sweet."**

Next.
I give you the gift of all gifts.
The gift of all the gifts
That you **never got."**
They are yours today.

Lastly,
I give you
The color Dark brown.
Like Your hair.
Long, Lovely.
Dark brown
Is what I see.
When I see you,
I see mom.
Happy Birthday.

Spring-Giavanna
(Giavanna reads below)

"Happy Birthday Mom,
I have three gifts for you.
The first gift is **you**, Mom.
You are a gift.
When I think of a gift
I think of You.
You are my mom.

The second gift is LOVE.
Wrapped in a Pink and Purple Dress,
With a diamond necklace for a bow.
With lots of chocolate as a surprise treat.
You love chocolate.

My last gift,
Are the colors Green and Brown.
Nature colors are gifts, too.

264

Leaves, trees, young mountains,
Coffee and chocolate brown.
Nature changes her colors
for you.
Happy Birthday, Mom.
I love you.

Summer-Natalia
(Natalia reads below)

"My three gifts honor your birthday.
My first gift is three words.
Kind and **Caring** and **Love.**
Because you are a **"GREAT"** mom.
You are kind.
And you are caring."

"My next gift is
A **check** for
Infinity Dollars - $$$$$$$...
Deposited in your own Bank Account."
"You deserve it.
You are a great mom to me
And my sisters."

"My third gift is the color **Pink.**
Pink is the color
Of **caring** and **kindness.**"
Happy, Happy, Birthday Mom

Fall-Graham
(Graham reads below)

"I too,
Come bearing
Three gifts
For your birthday.

My first gift is a word.
Audacious.
You were born
With a rare superpower.
The Willingness
To take
Surprising,
Bold Risks."

My second gift for you is…
Peace.
Simple and pure.
Peace.

My third birthday gift,
I give you a color.
The color of persimmons.

Permission grow
On trees of ebony.
Harvesting Edible fruit.
Sweet. Juicy.

Finger-licking Flavors.

Ripe Red, Yellow,
And Orange.
Soft, Sweet
Flavors Forever
Tickle your tongue.

These gifts we give to you.

We are your four seasons.
Winter, Spring, Summer, Fall.

Bringing you gifts for your

Seasons around the Sun."

Sir Duke's Alphabet
This poem is dedicated to Edward Kennedy Ellington

A song is Born
In My Garden of
African Flowers.

Your Soulful Spirit
Soars Silently
Across An African Jungle.
Affectionately Admiring
Antiquated Ashes,
Awful Sad.
Yet, Full of Anticipation.

Baby, When You Ain't There
All I Do Is Ballin' The Blues.
My Skin Sings Black, Brown and Tan
Blue and Green.

While Silently Shoutin'
Come On Home
Come On Home To The Cotton Club.

We Be Dancing On the Stars.
But.
Do Me A Favor Do Nothin' Til You
Hear From Me.
Dianah's In a Jam.

And I Got The Doghouse Blues.
You Know, I Don't Get Around Much Anymore
So.
Drop Me Off At Harlem, And Don't Ever
Say Goodbye.
Hey Baby, A Hundred Dreams Ago,
And A Handful of Haunted Nights,
You Hit Me With A Hot Note
And Watch Me Bounce.

It Will Be A Happy Reunion
A Hundred Dreams From Now.

I Let
A Song Out Of My Heart.
In Between a Mellow Tone.
It Ignites Into A Sentimental Mood.
I Illuminate In My Solitude.

I Got It Bad Y'all.
And That Ain't Good.
So. Suddenly It Jumped.
Somewhere A Strange Feeling
Slides in Slowly,
Like A Sun Swept Sunday,
On A Soul Soothing Beach.

She Sees. The Sultry Sunset's Silk Face
Slipping As The Sky Fell Down From
A Single Petal Of A Rose.

As three Black Kings. The Tele Casters.
Take The "A" Train.
You Better Take Time To Tune Up.
Before Tootin' Through The Roof.
With Your Timeless Trumpet in Spades.

It's Ten Past Twilight Time.
Time To Tell Me The Truth.
Tell Me. Tell Me The Truth.

To Know You Is To Love You.
To Know You Is To Love You.
Undaunted. Undeniable. Unquestioned.
The Unbooted Character
Of the United Brotherhood.
Walking and Singing The Blues.
Asking…

What Am I Here For?
What Am I To Do?
What Color is Virtue?
When I Walk With You?
Will You Be There?
You? You? You?
Will You Be There?
You of All People? Will You Be There?

Sisters

Sisters
one plus one plus one
equals
three
Single spirits standing alone.

Pure and Perfect
Clandestine Clues
Hidden Hollow Hints
Dancing.
Singing harmonies
Sweet. Savory. Spicy.
Blending separately together.
Becoming…
Pickett Puzzle
Pieces
Unknown Endings.
Triad Trilogies.
Mistaken Mysteries.
Invisible Identities.

No one knew who.
No one knew where.
No one knew why.
No one knew when
Childhood empty dreams
Captured stolen memories.
His presence

Captured in their smiles.

Chocolate and Caramel dreams.
Frozen forgotten futures.
Three Handfuls
and
Half a century
Of Belated Birthdays.
Suddenly Solved
One Spring Day in May
Not that long ago.

One story.
One song.
Three sisters.
One cast of thousands.
One internet ending.
Three journeys converge.

Into one fantastic Voyage.
Beginning. Ending.
With a weathered, wintery,
Faraway Familiar Smile
Wearing smooth suede shoes
With silk socks.
Dropping DNA
In the
Local Lost and Found.

Jean wares Mary Jane Shoes
With Winter White socks.
Barbara fears when the lights go out.
Enid hears jazz in the sunlight.

All different.
All the same.
His presence
Shadowed in their smiles.

Some say.
Seasons and Seconds
Play Hide and Seek
With Sankofa.

Some say,
They collide.
Into a net of Truth.

Some see.
Same eyes.
Same smile.
Same face.
Same father.

One plus one
Plus one
Equals three Sisters.
Once Lost.
Now Found.

Together for the first time.
His presence
Shadowed in their smiles.

Sitting in an empty parking lot

Sitting in an empty parking lot
under a lamp post
dimly lit.
Listening to jazz
quietly
humming
in my ears.
As…my…fingers
feverously find the places
where your magic spell unlocks
the most hidden memories of your
touch.
Touching…yourtouching…mytouching.
This Black magic potion
reveals the only hidden
true treasures
where All secrets,
All truths, All sacred joys
are sensuously celebrated.
As my long,
deep,
slender
messengers
send shock waves
through the bottom of
my
Endless pit of desires.
My fingers

play me
like the rhythms
of a slow
sax
solo.

Echoing,
surrounding
me,
filling
me.
My heart beats.
The Quickening…is
Near.
My breath is fast.
I pant
with familiar pleasure.
Eyes closed.
Rocking and Swaying
Soon.
Hmmmmm.
Real soon.
Jealous Voyeur.
Mouth wet with Wild Wonder.
Yes.
Oh Yes.
My fingers fondly fuck me.
They travel like a beacons in the fog.
They slip and slide in search of sensuous dessert.

As I sit
in an empty parking lot
under a lamp post
dimly lit.

Songs

The Songs we Sing
Are not just Songs.
Our Voices are the
Ageless Echoes
Of our Ancestors.

We are their Fruit.
We are their
Roots
Rebellious.
Revolutionary.

Intertwined
In Their
Interrupted
Imaginations.

Dare to Dream
Daydreams.

Their Wise
Wild Wishes.

The Words We Sing.

They Sang.
While

Beaten.
Battered.
Black and Blue.

We
Stand
Humble.
Proud.

On Spiritual
Super-Sized
Shoulders.

Immortalize.

From
the Middle Passage
to Mississippi.

From Martinique
to Memphis.

Remember.

Musical Muscle Memories
Live in DNA.
Soft Tender.
Bold Black
Brain-Wave Beats.

We Sing.
We Hum.
We Shout.
We Dance.
We Feel.
We Know.

Yes.

We KNOW.

WE SING.
WE SING.
WE SING.

Sonny Buxton - The Holy Grail of Jazz

He said,

"Have you ever wanted "to look in the mirror of Jazz?"

"I think it was when "I first heard Jazz."

"Really Listened to it, I was Enamored."

"It was something I began to Witness."

"As time went on, I Thought, "MY GOD!"

'There's nothing more exciting than this Music."

"This African American Classical Music."

Sonny Buxton's Words Become Brain Seeds.

Your Rearview Overflowing Vision

Of Encyclopedic Knowledge,

Tales & Tea, Good & Bad, Funny & Sad,

The Unknown & Ugly of Jazz.

Your Multi-View Perspective Memory

Some Say, "Google of Jazz."

Some Say, "Sankofa of Jazz."

Looking Backwards to the Past.

Holding Future Histories.

Some Say, he is the "P.H.D. of J.A.Z.Z."

Some Say, "Griot of Jazz."

Witness & Historian of

BeBop & Jim Crow. Salt & Pepper Clubs.

Milestones & Pearls.

He was Billy Strayhorn's <u>Friend.</u>

Some Say, KCSM's Saturday Mornings

Sonny Buxton's Jazz Ritual

#BFF's Worldwide.

He Walked in their Blue Suede Shoes.

Ellington. Miles. Hampton.

While creating your own Path.

He sat at their knees.

He ran with Jazz G.O.A.T.S.

1920's 1930's 1940's 1950's 1960's...

And on & on Till the Break of Down.

Innovative & Original.

Black Intelligentsia. Defiant Risk Taker.

Spearheading Change Agent.

Beacon of Love & Truth.

Some Say, these are the

Building Blocks of...

Jazz & Mr. Sonny Buxton.

You said, *"If you pause for a Moment*

To Listen, Something

Might Come Through."

Mr. Sonny Buxton. You Came Through.

Jazz is...Still Coming Through.

Thank You

For Keeping Jazz Alive.

Thank You

For Making Us See

Jazz Through Your Eyes.

Soothe.

Soothe.
Velvet.
Thick.
So Thick
You can't sip
through a paper straw.
But you keep on trying and trying.
Suddenly,
Love Drops
Become Condensed Dewdrops.
Into, in through,
One Old, Olive & Orange Mist.
Ancient Angelic Ancestral.
Taste becomes Pleasure.
Sweat. Blood. Tears.
Signals send silent shock waves
through the new night air.
Igniting.
Inviting
Inner Visions
from Stolen Dreams.
Falling faintly.
Yet, ForEver Familiar.
Free.
Suddenly.
Without any warning
You feel a silence.
A delicate De'ja vu.

Sweeps across your smile.
5 Velvet Shadows
Slowly begin to Smother your skin.
48 Velvet Vibrations
Soothe & shutter your soul.
Muscle Memories dance.
 Exhale.
Just remembering
makes your Rain Bow Wet
with a kismet kiss.
A near missed first kiss.
Sends signals & footprints
found on fallen stars.
Onyx African Intimacy.
Cell2Cell
Skin2Skin.
Soothe.
No words spoken.
Solos of Sensual singing.
Silently
Serenading.
Harmonizing.
Caramelizing.
Tantalizing.
Tasting
Tender tracks of tears.
Passionfruit & Burnt Coconut.
Hidden flavors
tickle your tongue.
 A Bruised Blush

slides across your smile.
Soothe.
Soothe.
Exhale.
Soothe.

Stand in the Warmth of Tomorrow Suns

"Jazz speaks
For Life."
"Blues tells
Her stories.
SoulfullySad,
Sacrificing,
Sacred, Secret,
Strategic Successes.
Fragments From Life's Difficulties.

Musical Triplets
Jazz, Gospel, Blues
First cousins to Mama Africa.
 in through,
 Inside,
 inbetween,
 Incised intimacies.

Simmered slowly
 In Septembers' Summer sun.
Marinating magnificent,
Mathematical mysteries.

Blown through
Ancient temples of Tones.
Soul stirring saxophone solos.
Hummed into
"Dead Daydreamers
288

Dare to dream" dreams of Freedom.
Gasconade Guttural Groans
Serpentine Spirits songs.
Birthed into the
Hearts of Jazz GOATS
Today, yesterday, and tomorrow.

Cut from
Grandpa Buster's
Cotton cloth pockets.
Sewn into
Leggetha's wise
Warm, worn
Quilts hiding maps
Stuffed with seeds
From stolen dreams
Middle Passage passengers.
Poised praying,
Passionate possibilities.

They took the hardest,
Heaviest, hateful realities,
Put them
Into,
in through,
Inside,
in-between,
Incised intimacies.

Simmered slowly
In Septembers' Summer sun.
Marinating magnificent,
Mathematical mystery mazes.

Blown through
Ancient temples of Tones.
Soul stirring saxophone solos.
Hummed into three part harmonies of
hypnotic hollow havens.

Dead Daydreamers "dare to dream"
Dreams of Freedom.
Gasconade Guttural Groans into Grinds.
Seeds of Yesterday buried in the Blues.
Serpentine Spirits songs.
Russian Roulette LoveSongs.
Passed on and on and on
Birthed into the
Hearts of Jazz GOATS
Today, yesterday, and tomorrow.
Jazz riffs stitched with nine needles
Cut from
Grandpa Buster's
Cotton cloth pockets.
Sewn into
Leggetha's wise
Warm, worn
Quilts hiding maps
Stuffed with seeds

From stolen dreams.

They all followed that
North Star's path.

While Stardust fell
On their heads.
While Tracing footsteps and fear.

They made minds clean,
Clear, creative, conscious.
Miles, Coltrane, Ella,
Maya, Ta-Nehisi, Duke, and Destiny.

"They took Life
Offering No order
No meaning.

Created Order
Created Meaning
From simple seductive sounds
Through their instruments."

Imagine developing a
Critical mindset
Beliefs, Values,
Attitudes, Orthodoxies
Through the eyes of Sankofa.
 J a z z
Takes her first baby steps

She stumbles, She stands,
She struts,
She soars with stardust in her shoes.

She Continues her timeless tradition.
Singing songs from
More Complicated,
Contradicted, Confused
Urban existence.

"Change does not roll in
On wheels of inevitability,
But through continuous
Challenge and Controversy."

The Revolution was not televised.
She was <u>in</u> the recording studio.

Leaving Footprints,
Fingerprints
On wax, tape,
And digital dreams.

Bringing Bags, Bags,
And Bags of Bittersweet Beats.

"New Hope
With a
New Sense of Triumph.
Some call, "Triumphant Music."

Some say Black Music.

Some say,
Steppings Stones
Into Tomorrow.
Some say,
Infused voices
Waiting to be heard.

Young voices.
Gifted voices.
Shouting, chanting, singing.
"Ethnic Integrity."
"Ethnic Integrity."

The Future looks
Into the eyes
Of Tomorrow.

She Saw.
She knows.
Soulless Shadows of the past
Soon Slowly fades.

She saw Sanguine Sunsets.
Sagacious Sunrises.

Senseless
Soulless Spirits
With empty pockets

Slowly
Sadly Fade.

So. Choose.
Choose.
Choose The Sun's
Welcoming, Warm Wisdom.
Stand in
Rainbow rays
Of pregnant possibilities.

Or.
Stand in Saline shade.
Drink cold tasteless tea
Of Frosty Forgotten Dreams.
Feel her chill grow into night.

But Stand.
Stand.
Stand Tall.

Show them who you are.

Choose.
Stand.

Stand in the Warmth of Tomorrow Suns.
Stand in the Warmth of Tomorrow Suns.

Star Dust
A poem for Sierra

Star Dust

Ancient Ancestral
Tiny Travelers
Marching
Millions & Millions

Of Magical Mysterious
Mega Miles.
Deliberately Disguised as...Super Stars.

Their Cargo Carefully Combines
All Time & All Space.
They Fearlessly Form & Fall
From the New Night Sky.
One By One.
Knowing & Not Knowing
When or if to Land.
No One
Could Never
Ever Imagine
Your Journey
Sierra.

Arriving
Perfect.

Precise.
In...
My Heart.
My Life.
My Daughter.
My Deepest Dream
Come True.
You.

Sierra.
Sacredly Sculpted.
Forever Imperfectly
Imprinted.

Your Thoughts. Star Dust.
Your Dreams. Star Dust.
Your Strengths. Star Dust.
Your Words. Star Dust.
Your Breath. Star Dust.
Your Secrets.

All Are
Star Dust.

You are
The Essence of
Stars.

You are
The Essence of
You.

Twin Twinkling
Twilight Beams
Touch & Tickle.

Creating Every Star.
Every Comet. Every Moon Beam.
Every Planet's Cosmic Shadow of
Every Infinite Atom.

All Are You.

You Are Star...Dust...
You... Are... Starrrrrrr...Dust.

Sugar Pie De Santo
Queen of the West Coast Blues

In the Kingdom of The Harlem Renaissance

Of the West

Reigned Three Queens.

The First Queen Born. Queen Sugar Pie De Santo.

Sweet Black Fierce Filipina.

Named "Sugar Pie" By the Great Johnny Otis.

Your Fingerprint Sings Chocolate City.

Sexy. Gritty.

Queen Sugar Pie De Santo Penned over

One Hundred Musical Compositions.

Many landed on the R & B charts.

Slip-n-Mules. Use What You Got. I Want You.

Do I Make Myself Clear?

I Don't Want to Fuss.

Where can you party all Night Long?

Queen Sugar Pie De Santo Knows.

Party in The Basement with Cousin Miss Etta James.

1959. You Opened & Toured

With the Great Godfather of Soul in

The James Brown Revue.

Doesn't Get Any Better Than That.

You wrote, *"I played a Losing Game*

Life Goes on Just the Same."

Worthy Words of Wisdom

Stronger than a Hurricane

Blowing Away your Heart & Soul.

Volcanic Vocals Takes You

To Church Every Time. Baptized in The Bay.

Foot Stomp-in' Juke Joint R & B

Rock Me Baby

Grabs You where You Forgot

"How Good" It Can Feel.

Live Performances all "On Fire."

Leaving the stage…Feet Still Smokin'.

Josephine Baker & Lottie the Body Can't Hold a Candle

To Your Moves.

Fearlessly Brave Brutally Honest

No Joke for a Black Woman Artist

During The Civil Rights Era.

You Paid your Dues. Packed Your Power

By the Square Inch.

Accolades from Ancestors

Musical Gifts & Lifetime Achievement Awards.

In the Western Kingdom of the

Harlem Renaissance

Queen Sugar Pie Crowned

Queen of the West Coast Blues.

Best Female Blues Singer

Bay Area Music Awards.

You Touched that Apollo Tree Stump

Over Twenty Times.

That's not All.

Band Leader. Songwriter.

Dancer. Producer.

Vocalist. Consummate Artist.

History Knows Your Name.

Whispering Walls at

The Fillmore & The Sportsman

Say, "Thank You

Miss Sugar Pie De Santo."

You Made it Clear

You Made it Crystal Clear.

Your "Bad Ass" Blues will Rock Forever.

Sweet Dreams Sweet Realities

Sweet Dreams.
Sweet Realities.
Your Wishes are Waiting.
For You.
Send Them Off.
On the Backs of a Whisper.
Imagine.
How They will Fly Back
Into Your World.
With Love.
Gratitude.
Pass it On.
You will See.
They Will Come Back to You.
Again.
And Again.

Images created by Article3.org for the 75th Anniversary of the Universal Declaration of Human Rights

304

The Quilt

This Quilt is 75 years old.
Each piece
Traveled around many Suns.
Some from faraway
Villages
To the
World Wide Web.
Each piece
Embedded in History.
This quilt is Unique.
This quilt is Universal.
This Quilt…
Pauses,
Ponders,
Reflects,
Fearlessly Focuses on
Defining
Issues
From Our time.
From Our Time.
Today.
December 2023.

This Quilt
Conceived.
Created with
Bountiful
Bold

Beautiful,
Threads,
Strings,
Ribbons,
Selflessly Sharing
Stitched Struggles and Songs.

Each piece. A Voice.
An Unapologetic Voice.
Transforming Harmonies
Singing Solos.

Each piece
created
By Artists/Activists
Daily Documenting
Our Living History.
Kehinde Wiley,
Rosa Lee Tompkins
Angela Davis
BTS.

Each piece personally picked.
Pastoral. Pictorial, Political.
Pleasing Pieces, Pleading Pieces
Praying Pieces.
From Every Human Struggle.
This Quilt
Stitched with Nine Naked Needles
Naming

the
Newest Members
to the
Fastest Growing
Global Phenomena.
"The Climate Change Gang"
Chad
Democratic Republic of Congo
Somalia
Afghanistan
Central African Republic
Nigeria
Ethiopia
Syria
South Sudan and
Bangladesh.

Listen.
This piece Sings.
Keffiyeh is Singing.
They Sing
Songs of Struggle /Songs of Hope.
Songs of Life and Liberty.

Tenderly Touch this Piece
Taken from
Ten Thousand T-Shirts
Off Unbought, Unbossed Backs
of The United Auto Workers.

Calmly Caress
Crème Colored Cashmere
Socks Swatches.
Soft socks with Baby Ducks.
Stained Pink.
From Running. Running.
Running **For** Your Life.
Running **To** Freedom.
Running **From**
Torture. Trafficking.

Sunlight Fades.
Slowly
Staining Shadows
on
Hand-picked Cotton Corners
Dancing in the wind.
Welcoming Spring.
A hint of Mint.
A Hair Ribbon.
Last seen.
On a doll.
Torn. Worn from War.
Somewhere between
Russia and Ukraine.
She
Double Vision Dreams
Searching for Candy, and Conflict Resolution.

This Quilt

Shouts Out to:
All Oppressed
To
All Freedom Fighters.

Shout Outs to:
All
H U E M A N S Rights
H U E M A N

This Quilt
Holds
Five Flavors of Freedom
whereas
All Human Rights are
Inherent to us all.
Regardless of Nationality
Sex, Gender, National Ethnic Origin/Color
Religion. And Language

This Quilt Celebrates
75 Years of Human Rights.
Honoring and Upholding

1 The Right **to** Life and Liberty.
2 The Right **to** Education.
3 Freedom **from** Slavery and Torture.
4 Freedom **of** Opinion and Expression.
5 Freedom **to** Work.

75 Pieces. One Quilt.
Each piece
Traveled around many Suns.
Each piece
Embedded in History.
This Quilt is Unique.
This Quilt is Universal.
This Quilt
Pauses
Ponders,
Fearlessly Focuses.
On Defining issues
From our time.

From Our Time
Today.
December 2023.

The Universal Irony

The Classic Karmic Lesson.
How Death Touches Life.
The Life of Spirit.
The Life is Spirit.
The Energy of Breath.
LifeForce.
It Embraces you.
Comforts the Heart.
Healing Itself.
With Grief.
The Lost is Found.
Via Transformational Change.
It's True.
Octavia E. Butler.
She knew.
God is Change.
Change is God.
It's True. I was there.
My friend, Debbie Davis
Shared the Secret of Being
Closer To Free.
We waited. We watched.
We touch the hem of Death
Fearlessly.
As you felt the Silences between
The Presence.
The Soft Dignity of It's Touch
Transforms you.

You go far Beyond
You go Deeper,
Beyond
Your Wildest Dreams.
You. Like the Velveteen Rabbit
Actually Do BECOME REAL.

Three Voices Three Poems Three Sisters
Prologue

Three Voices.
Three poems.
Three Sisters.

Sophia. Natalia. Giavanna.

Insightful & Intelligent.
One Smile.
One Joy.
One Bond.
One Heart.

Three Sisters' Superpower.
Rival the Avengers
& Wonder Woman.

Music.
Their Secret Language.
Unspoken.
Unbroken.

Harmonizing Effortlessly.
Empathetically Together.
They Know.
Yes.
They Know.

Three Voices.
Three Poems
Three Sisters.

Make Three Wishes.
Your Next Adventure Awaits.

Three Sisters Poem One Sophia

Poem One
Sophia

Three Voices.
Sisters Harmonizing.
Over Morning Oatmeal.

Drawing & smiling.
Writing & coloring.
Thinking...
Yelling & playing.
Running & singing.
Thinking...

Listening & speaking.
Crying & laughing.
Reading & dreaming.
Thinking & creating.

All At the Same Time.

Pokemon.
Sonic & Steven Universe
Wish they were
Wild & Worldly,
Wonderfully Wise
Beyond their Youth.
Like Sophia, Natalia, And Giavanna.
Three Voices.

Three Beautiful
Bittersweet
Sisters.

Firstborn.
Sophia
Warmly Welcomed Winter.
Majestic Stoic Eyes Sees Far Into
Your Soul.

Your Future.
Your Heart.
Your Words.

Halfway around the Sun
She Sang her first Song.
Eight Times Around
She Wrote Her First Book.

Imagination Explorer Extraordinaire.
Discovering Insights, Intuition, Implicitness.
Promises & Principles.

Watching & Waiting
One Voice Becomes Two.
Two Voices Soon Become Three.
Big Sister's New BFF is "Patience."

Sophia Gifts Decoded
Inside a Magical Maze.
She.

Alone Unlocks the Doors
Her Limitless Innovative Imagination.
Unseen by Most.

Tall Oaks Communicate
Sharing One Complex & Hidden
Underground Root Community.

Sophia Sprouted Roots First.
First to Know
Her Core.
Her Journey
& Her World.

Angels harmonize
When she sings.
Adroit Artists
Know her Masterful art.

Kindheartedness her
Key That Opens all her doors.
A Reader's Delight
Makes any library blush.

Ask Sweetie Bell.
She knows.
She knows.
She knows
Her Love.
She knows.

Her tender touch.
Her Calming Secret Song.

Big Sister Sophia.
Loving Sister.
She Understands.

Stand Sophia.
Stand Tall.
Stand Strong.

Show Them Who You Are.

Three Sisters Poem Two Natalia

Poem Two
Natalia

Flew In
On the Bright Side
of a Winter's Breeze.
Warm & Soft.
Calm & Intuitive.
Bundle of J.O.Y.
Born Down Under.
On A Hot Winter
Australian August Sky.

Natalia.

Knew Sophia's Voice
Before She was Born.
She Silently Sang with her.

Natalia.

Ready to Begin.
Ready to Be
With her sister.
Ready to See her Voice.

Natalia.

Thinking Before
She Was Born.
She Danced
To Her Mother's Heartbeat.
Soon...
They would Sing Effortlessly.
Blending Voices & Tones.

Natalia.

Fierce & Independent.
Clear Concise Communicator.
An Equal Opportunity Sister.
Tender Heart Strength.
Social Justice Baby.

Calling Out #UnFairness. #Injustice.
With her Sweet Toothless Smile.

Born to Learn & Lead.
Born to Compete to Win.
Born to Glue Together Missing Ends.
Born to Loyally Love her Family.

She Listens with
Kind Heart & Wise Soul
Armed with Intelligence & Passion.

Ready & Determined
To Defend & Fight For her Truth
By Any Means Necessary.

Art & Music
Her Tools & Toys.
Memory & Understanding Her Guides.
She says,
"I am in the Middle.
Sophia is First.
Giavanna is Third."

Natalia.

Claims & Holds
Her Status Early.
Truth Teller for her sisters.
Truth Slips & Slides
A Bit Sometimes.

Natalia.

Stand Natalia.
Stand Tall.
Stand Strong.

Show Them Who You Are.

Three Sisters Poem Three Giavanna

Poem Three
Giavanna

Born In Late Spring.
Birds Sang
Of her Arrival

"Giavanna is here."
"Giavanna is here."

Springtime...
Nature's Favorite
Flower Show Season.
Displaying
All
Her
Favorite
Colors.

Giavanna
Born Sliding on a Rainbow.
Fearless and Free.

AKA GiGi.

Youthful Shade
Of Fairy Mint Green.
Overshadowed With Wisdom.

Paints with All Her Colors.
Pink & Unicorn,
Her Favs.

Abundant Seeds of Thought.
Abundant Grace.
Abundant Energy.
Abundant Giggles.
GiGi Races to
Welcome Her Sisters
Voices & Songs
In Three Part Harmony.

I bet, GiGi
Talked to Them
In Her Mama's Belly.
Negotiating & Debating,
Theorizing.
The Seven Wonders of the Universe.
The Laws of Life.
All At the Same Time.

GiGi's Way...
Short Sweet & Simple.

GiGi's Gifts Opened Early.
Third but first.
Her Superpowers Too Many
To List.

Adorned
With Imagination & Language.
Born a Word Smith
With A Silver Tongue.
With Multisyllabic Words.
Diagnostic Quick Wit.
She Knows.
You Go Girl!

Stand Giavanna.
Stand Tall.
Stand Strong.

Show Them Who You Are.

Three Titans
25th Anniversary of Healdsburg Jazz Festival

Jazz Titans
Cedar, Bobby, Billy.
Cedar Walton, Bobby Hutcherson, Billy Higgins
Collided at the
Keystone Korner
in North Beach
With *Jazz in Flight*
JessicaJazz
Co-pilot.
Aficionado.

Kaleidoscopic night vision
Polaris plan was poised.
Stars…aligned.
Moon…full.
Destiny…foretold.
A dream fantastic.
The Story begins.
As
Friends.
Jazz Angels
In Hueman skin.
Common denominator
Lovers of J A Z Z.
Smoke streams simmering
Hot from Eddie Moore's
Jazz Festivals founded by

JessicaJazz.
Kissed by Kismet
They landed.
In a small sleepy town
In the North Bay.
Healdsburg, CA.

Footprints Found
In Healdsburg Plaza.
Glimmers gently faded & flickered.
From the Raven Theater.
If those walls could talk,
Jazz Heaven would blush.

A Jazzy Dream was conceived.
A Community festival founded by Friends.
1999 Maiden Voyage
Three days in June
Raven Performing Arts Theater
The Three Titans
Cedar, Billy, and Bobby
Performed Perfection

Billy Higgins told JessicaJazz
"If you educate the kids,
You will secure.
The future of Jazz."

Visionary Dreams and Seeds
Sprouted Operation Jazz Band.

Local students listening & performing.
With Jazz GOATS.

Turn Around and it's
The Year 2000
Pregnant with infinite possibilities
The World took notice.
Imagine Jazz Artists
From Sebastopol to Bombay.
Twenty trips around the sun.
Following Footsteps into the future.

Turn Around Twice it's
The Year 2020.
Healdsburg Jazz
Took a leap of Faith.
Marcus Shelby named.
The New "Artistic Director"
Pockets packed with
Artists in Residents
Tammy Hall, Destiny Muhammad,
John Santos, photographer, George Wells,
Even A Jazz Poet Laureate.

Imagine Listening to
A Freedom Jazz Choir
Singing Harriet Tubman
With Tiffany Tunes.

Jazz GOATS

Humming at the
Healdsburg Hotel
Sipping world class wines.

It's not a dream.
It's a dream come true.

Thank You JessicaJazz.

"Concise Connections
Networking Notes.
Rhythms Fly.
On Backs of
Whimsical Wicked Winds.
That's JessicaJazz.
Billy Higgins *Soweto*
Charles Lloyd
Forest Flowers
Planted Forever.
Syncopated Soldiers in
JessicaJazz's
Musical Army.
They Proudly Pour
Their Hearts Out
Playing Pure Patterns
Of Sacred Sankofa.

Young Minds Meld
Into Old.
Touched By her Magic.

She *sees* far
Into Futures.
She *hears* Echoes.
Endless singing.
JessicaJazz.
JessicaJazz.
JessicaJazz.

Let **Us** give thanks,
Let **Us** give love,
Let **Us** give gratitude.
To those who blessed **Us**
With their Artistic Grace.

I present to you today.
The 25th Anniversary
Of the Healdsburg Jazz Festival.

The Legendary Hall of Fame
The Silver Honor Roll
Of Jazz GOATS
AKA Jazz Heaven
1999-2023

 Healdsburg's JAZZ HEAVEN

The Titans of Jazz
~Billy Higgins,
~Bobby Hutcherson,
~Cedar Walton,

~Abbey Lincoln,
~Charlie Haden
~Joey DeFrancesco
~Pharoah Sanders
~Von Freeman
~John Abercrombie
~Henry Butler

All Playing together
In Jazz Heaven forever.

Two Voices
A poem dedicated to Dr. Martin Luther King, Jr.

Shhh. Shhh.
Listen.
Listen with your eyes.
See. See with your ears.
Sankofa Signals
Sends a single, sweet, singing shockwave
 Melting millions of sounds,
words, songs. cries, whispers.

Each Echoing
the first word,
the first cry,
the first song.

Shhhh, Shhhh
Do you hear
Do you hear
What I hear?
I hear
*Injustice **anywhere** is a **threat***
*To justice **everywhere**.*

I hear
we are caught
Caught in an inescapable network of mutuality,
Tied in a single garment of Destiny."

Do you see
What I see ?

Yes, I see.
I see
That *"Darkness*
Cannot drive out darkness;
*Only **light** can do that.*
I see
hate cannot drive out hate;
*Only **love***
Can do that."

No, No.
Not me.

I don't see.
I don't see
"The ultimate measure of a man
Is not where he stands
In moments
Of comfort and convenience,

But
where he stands
At times
Of challenge and controversy."

Do you feel?
Do you feel?

What I feel?
Do you feel?
A true revolution of values
will **soon** cause us
To **Rise** Up
To **Wake** Up
To **Question**
The **fairness** and **justice**
Of many of our
past and present policies?

Do you feel
That **true** compassion
Is more,
Much, much more
Than flinging a coin to a beggar?
Or
Do you **question** *why*,
Why do beggars **exist?**

Do you **really feel**
There are times
to **recognize**

When a man made law
Is **totally out** of harmony,
Out of balance,
Out of control,

Out of reality,
with the moral law of the universe?

Do you hear what I hear?
See what I see?

Feel
What I feel?

Do you know
What I know?

I know
*"Like life,
racial understanding
is not something
that we **find**
Not something you stumble across,
but
Something we must create."*

No. No.No.
I don't
I don't know.
I don't **want** to know
I don't want to know

That *"until the Blackman gets Free,
Whitemen will not B Free."*

Do you trust
What I trust?

Do you trust that
*"The **arc** of the moral universe*
is long, long, lingeringly long
But
It beautifully bends towards
Justice."

Do you care?
That *"now*
Right NOW
Is the time.
The time
To lift our national policy from the
Quicksand of racial injustice
To the solid, steady, solid rock
Of Human Dignity?"

Do you hear what I hear?
See what I see?
Feel
What I feel?

Do you sing?
Songs
Our
Ancestors sang?
Free At Last.

Free At Last
Thank God,
Thank God,
Almighty,
We
Are Free
At Last?"

And…
Do you love?
What I love?

Do you **love** that
When the history books
Are written in the future,
Somebody will have to say
Somebody will have to say

"There lived a race of people…
Who had the moral courage
*To **Stand Up***
And Fearlessly Fight
For their rights."

Or…Or…Or
Do you love that
When the history books
Are written in the future
Somebody will have to say
There lived a race of people

Who **did not**
Could not
Would not have
The moral courage
To Stand Strong
To Stand Up
To Stand Proud
To Fear less ly Fight
For Their Rights?

Free Will is always Free.
Free Will is…always Free.

Do you sing?
Do you see?
Do you hear?
Do you feel?
Do you fight?
Do you know?
Do you trust?

Do you love?

Ujima

Today, Yesterday, and Tomorrow
We...Honor Ourselves
We...Love Ourselves
We...Celebrate Ourselves
We...Remember Ourselves
with Kwanzaa.

1966
A community leader and educator created Kwanzaa.
He wanted to help African-Americans remember
The rare, rich, reality of our
African-American heritage.

His name, Maulana Ron Karenga.
Brother. Genius. Black Man Magik.
He gave us 7 days and 7 nights of "US"
With exquisite, expressive exercises
That begins with the Kinara
Swahili for candleholder.

Each night symbolically rekindles our
Past and Present
Principles coded in
Red. Green. Black.

Our homemade holiday of
History, Love,
And Remembrance with a purpose.
That Purpose
to Pass Kwanzaa on to our babies, babies, babies.

Today is day 3.
Ujima
Collective Work Responsibility
So, let's talk about
Collective Work Responsibility.

We. People of Africa
Are born with the DNA
Collective Work Responsibility.
Our Ancestors were True
Tribal Sustainable Geniuses
For thousands and thousands of years.
Creating FuFu to temples in
Timbuktu, Egypt, and South Africa.
Did you know?
Egyptian temples were also economically significant to
Egyptian Civilization?

Where do y'all think trade came from?

Collective Work and Responsibility
Is the first foundation of all people of Africa.
It took and is still taking over

400 years of lies and false advertising to
Directly erase our truth of collective work and responsibility.

So, let's talk about our Truth here in the USA.
My family tree is your family tree.
My family. Your family. Our family.
Strange fruit on our family tree.

That tree still has its roots buried into our yesterdays and
todays.

Remember?
The Green Book by Victor Hugo Green?
Collective Work Responsibility
Remember the Black Renaissance?
Collective Work Responsibility
Remember the Black Book by Toni Morrison?
Collective Work Responsibility
Remember 1921? Black Wall Street?
AKA Greenwood Oklahoma?
Collective Work Responsibility
Remember 1923? Rosewood, Florida?
A town so strong, they destroyed it just for existing.
Remember Black Lives Matter?
Collective Work Responsibility

Remember?
Every Black Community Center, every Black Juke Joint,
Every Black Storefront Church, every Black Barber Shop &

Black Beauty Shop? On the corner?
That's Collective Work and Responsibility.

True. They are almost all gone.
Due to:
Integration,
Red Lining,
Miseducation
Sundown Codes,
Being in Black Skin, and
Gentrification.

And in full, open oppressive
Spitefulness towards
People of Africa
We are Surviving systemic
Racism and Oppression.
They thought we would all die.
African People will never die.
We continue to outlive and outlast...

Surreal Strange Fruit
Spies in the Parlor with secrets and lies.
Snakes in white robes and so called "rights"

We survive. We sustain. We soar. We succeed. We see. We
school. We shout. We share. We sing. We show up. We serve.
We shine. We swagger. We sacrifice. We stay.

We self-determine our
Collective Work Responsibility
We Honor.
We Love.
We Celebrate.
We Remember...
Ujima.

We Are

We are Electric VisionVibrations.
We are StarDust.
We are Water.
We are Sound.
Vibrating into endless eternal voids of Harmony.

We Are
DreamSeeds Holding
Magical Mystical Maps of Insight.
We Are
Shadows Warm with Wisdom and Whispers.
We Are
Distant yet Far
Like the Black of your hand.

We Are
Omnipotent Memory Maps.
We Are
Unlimited,
Unending, Unbreakable
Promises.

We Are
The Daydreams of the Dead.
Buried with Blueprints
Of Intimate Insightful Inner Vision.
We Are
Dark Daring Diamond Discoveries

Waiting. Waiting. Waiting.

For
Your Tender Touch.
Your Infinite Intelligence
Your Innate Intuition.

We Are
Majestic Mythical Memory Melodies.
Singing
Sacred Silent Sounds.
We Are
Unborn Waiting.
We Are
BabySteps
To the Future.
We Are
Written on the Black
Of your Soul.

We Are
Wet Glistening Raindrops
Wanting to become Rainbows.

We Are Hope.
We Are Love.
We Are Fearless.

We Are
Dancing

On the edge of eternity
Ready to jump.
And look up.

Wet Dream Drops

Sheets Cool. Patiently...
Privately Pleading...
Calm with Anticipation Ready with Resolve

Waiting...Wishing...Wanting... Your body Heat
Your Dry Sauna Body Heat Suddenly sizzling

Steam Drops so Wet.

My Lover and I Sleep Together
In Separate Beds...

Breathe.
Slow...
Exhale.
Now Exhale Again. Find yourself Deepening

Into Desire. Spiritual.
Sensual.
Silence
Senses your Scent.

Mouth and other portals Tingle. Tickle.
Tasting Your
Wet Dream Drops.

We Dream Together.
We Make Cream Together.

My Lover and I Sleep Together
In Separate Beds.

Reaching Arms

With Musical Memory of Search Lights
On a cloudy Full Moon night.

They Know... They Move... Perfectly. Precisely. Penetrating.

Yes. I know.
This Meaning.
This Muscle Memory Meaning.

Heart Beats
Slow Dance Together Synchronized Swimmers In Sex Wet
Water.

Yes, I Can Hear...
Your Thoughts.
"You'll cum soon...soon."

Millions of muscles release at the same time. Stretching.
Reaching.
Your Constant Constellation of Stars. Aquarius.

The Water Bearer.

Star Dust Falls When We Climax
Our Body Heat Sends Shock Waves
Into The Future.

Our Body Heats Faster
Than the Speed of Light.

My Lover and I Sleep
In Separate Beds. Together

What Kind of Ancestor Are You Going to Be?

What kind of Ancestor
are you going to be?

What colors will be added
to this tapestry of Sankofa?

What stories
will be
written memories
marbled in
marigold margins
of majestic mountains?

What shadows will rest
on shoulders of secret silence,
sore, yet sentimental?

Whose words will
Forever
faithfully follow you
into forgotten corners
frozen in time?

What smiles will sing
deep down in your
destiny DNA
waiting,
waiting ?

What echoes will haunt you
sliding on sunbeams
in midday July heat
during a lightning storm
riding rainbows?

What dreams
will be inviolate
pure, presteen
holding,
holding
hard
onto
morning moist dew
wet with early edges
the first drops
in between
the pulse of morning and tomorrow?

What tree
will feed you
fresh flawless
fruit of the future?

What stardust
will fall
on your head
with icy white whispers
disguised as
Winter Wisdom?

What footsteps stained
with kitchen grease and Gumbo
will dance to the beat
of the Summer of Soul
1969 Harlem,
forgotten and found
like our history?

What blueprints will
you sew in
Your Grandmother's quilt?

What tastes will never
forget what it tasted
just one time?

What roots
Do not know
What a leaf
Has in mind?

What passionate, powerful,
shea butter salve
will heal your heavy heart
bruised by darkness?

What songs will you sing
in the shallow caves
of centuries?

What voyager's path will be
marked by the stars
not the sand dunes?

Whose children will be knighted
Young Gifted and Black?

What poems will be shaped
into bones
to stand tall on
Sadden shoulders?

What stone in the river
knows how thirsty the hill is?

What daydreams
coded into seeds
will be planted
on slave castle shores
drunk with death?

Answers
Answers you want
Answers you need
Answers you crave
Answers you seek
my friend
are not
mysteries.

You will find it…
You will find it
in a place,

A place you already know
A place you've never seen.

A place inside you
A place
that you must keep
Safe,
inviolate,
clear

So, nobody,
nobody
Will ever
Ever
Invade,
invalidate,
impede.

A place…
where
no one will
Curse you
no one will
hurt you
no one will
not see you.

A place where trust and truth are twins.

A place where
No one will ever
Treat you badly
in any,
any,
anyway…

A place with
Wise, Warm,
worldly wishes
are waiting
to welcome you.
Home.

What words
will you speak
When you meet
them All?

They are Waiting for us
They are Welcoming us
They are Singing our names

Home
Asking

What kind of Ancestor
are you going to be?

What Would Dr. Martin Luther King, Jr. Do?

Would he return his Nobel Peace Prize?
Where would he find Peace today?
Would he speak out against War?
Would Love still be his message?

Would he speak up for those who suffer?
Would those who suffer stand up for him?
Would he trust the courts?
What would he do about gun violence?
Would he trust the media?

What would he say about mass incarceration?
Who would be his trusted advisers?
Would he be a capitalist?
Would he burn down hatred?

Would he love Hip Hop and Jazz?
Would he destroy ignorance?
Would greed tempt him?
Would he be harassed by the FBI?
What would he say to Malcolm?

How would he define
What it means to be fully human?
Who would he name as the oppressor?
Would he help those who are being oppressed?

What Would Dr Martin Luther Jr. Do?

Would he build our economy with jobs?
What would he say about
Palestine? Sudan? Haiti? Ukraine? Israel?
Would he trust his own government?
Would the government trust him?

Which world leaders would stand with him?
Would ghetto streets and parks honor his name?
What would he say about immigration and the Wall?
Which Black leaders would turn their backs?

Would he talk about Peace on
TikTok and Instagram?
Who would follow him?
Who would protect him?
Would violence shut him down with silence?

Would he march in the Gay Pride Parade?
Would Union workers march with him?
Would he redistribute economic and political power?
Would the Black Church vilify him?
Consider him a saint or a sell out?

What would encourage him?
What would he say to his grandchildren?
What lessons would his sermons teach?
Would his dream still be a dream?

**<u>Do you know</u> what
Dr. Martin Luther King Jr. Would Do Today?**

Would he read the books that are banned?
Would his own country consider him a dangerous man?
Where would he feel safe and free?

Would the South Betray him?
Would the North Extort him?
Would the East Ignore him?
Would the West Sabotage him?

Who would sing his favorite hymn?
Would the police protect him?
Would he vote for Public Healthcare?
What would he say to Coretta?

Will his words be remembered? Or...
Will his words ignite a movement?
What would social media say about him?

Would he inspire YOU to
March, Sing, Stand, Sit, Sacrifice?
Would he be respected and revered?

What would Dr. Martin Luther King Jr.
Do For You?
And What would You
Do for him?

White Supremacy is neither white or supreme. Poem for John William Coltrane 2

Before
White
Was Supreme.

Before
1900
Met 26.

Before
Destiny's Door
Danced

With
Church Blues
Harmonizing
Middle Passage
Moans.

A
Dark Skinned
Daring,
Deferred Dream

Was Conceived.
Somewhere on a
Mint Green

Spring *Equinox* Night
Not…that long ago.

Imagine…
Lava Stars Dust
Whispering with Black Blood Drops.

Imagine…
Mere Monumental Moments
Of Sacred
Bruised Brilliancy
After the Rain.

Imagine…
Silent Shadows at the Village Gate
Sliding smiles on the Faces of the Dead.

This **Being of Human**
Scarred with
Spiritual Dirt
On his fingers
Was Named
John William Coltrane.

Spiritual
Sensual
SaxSoulful
Stirring Sounds.
Vibrations. Murmurations.
Intimately, Silently sending

Auras of Audibility.

Pure.
Infinite.
Lyrical Libations of Liberations.

In a
Moment's Notice,
Complete Timeless Convergence.
Into Immaculate Colored Conception - J A Z Z.

Where All Senses
Physical & Spiritual Eclipse
Into
My One and Only Love.

John William Coltane
Giant's Steps Surrounded you
Dizzy, Ornette, Miles, Ella,
Naima, Blue Train,

The Last Poets,
Pharaoh, McCoy, Elvin,

Alice & Ravi.

Coltrane is **Jazz**.

Coltrane is…
Raw.

Rogue.
Righteous.
Revolutionary Rhythms.

Coltrane is…
Interstellar
In Through
Timeless Transformations.

Into…
Something Magical.
Into Something Mystical.
Into Something Beyond Spiritual.
Something Ancient.
Something Supreme.

My One and Only Love.

My Words
Lost and Found
Lie Limp
Longingly Leaving
Ten Thousand
Tiny Tarnishes.

My Words
Inadequately Shy.
Bite their Tongues.

Unmasking Muscle Memory
Muse *Impressions*
Of Your *SummerTime* Finale.

You said…

*"I know
that there are
bad forces.*

*Forces
that bring suffering
to others.
And misery to the world."*

You said…

*"I WANT TO BE
The opposite force.
I WANT TO BE
The force
which is
Truly
For
GOOD."*

John William Coltrane
This Force is
Clearly **YOU.**

Your Name
Born *in* Afro Futures.
Born Whispering Miracles.
Born with Secrets in the soles of your shoes.
Born with Ancestor Seeds in your pocket.
Born with the Universe in your mouth.

With the Universe in your mouth.

Your Avant-Garde Jazz
Made love to Forbidden Siren Songs.

John William Coltrane
Jazz **Sings**
Your Name.

Jazz **Sings**
Your Name.

We **Love**
All Your
Favorite Things.

We **See**
Cosmic Jungles on
African Cave Dwellings.

We **Hear**
Echoes of Unborn Spirits.
Remembering Juke Joints

Covered in red muddy rain.

We **Watch**
Your words
Cakewalk down Hamlet streets.

We **Remember**
"Your voice
At the Mercy
Of its own Power."

We **Remember**
"Your voice
At the Mercy
Of its own Power."

JohnWilliamColtrane.
AKA. JazzGoat.

AKA…
Forever.
Forever.
Forever.

Why?
This circle poem is dedicated to our children.

We allegedly pledge our antiquated anti-defamed allegiance
to america. Why?

We callously convert our cataract compartmentalized courage
to a confused CARELESS country that cries Christian carols
constantly of fear. Why?

We secretly shamelessly share our collective cognitive
dissonance. Why?

We aimlessly chase our contradictions like **zombies** buying
millionaire lottery tickets with food stamps. Why???

We dream the same dream. Why?
We eat the same food. Why?
We buy the same trick. Why?
We reread the same sound bite.
We medicate the same dis-ease.
We use the same soap

That will never, ever, ever **ever**
clean the stain of quantum hate and deafening fear.

We live on the same rock separated isolated alone?
We kill children.
We kill our children?

We... kill...children?
wekillourchildren?
Why??
We can't breathe the same air.
Why???
why?
why?

Because
We...allegedly pledged our antiquated anti-defamed
allegiance to america.
Because we callously converted our cataract
compartmentalized courage to a confused CARELESS country
that cries christian carols constantly of fear.
Why?

Because
we secretly shamelessly shared our collective cognitive
dissonance.

Because
we aimlessly chased our contradictions like zombies buying
millionaire lottery tickets with food stamps.

Because
we dreamt the SAME dream.

Because
we ate the SAME food.
we bought the SAME trick.

Because
we read and reread the SAME sound bite.

Why?
Because
we medicated the SAME dis-ease.

Because
we used the SAME soap
That will never
EVER, EVER, EVER
cleanse the stain of quantum hate and deafening fear.

Because
we lived on the SAME rock separated isolated ALONE.

Because
we shared the SAME forgotten nightmarish memory.

Because we killed our children,
Because we...........
killed
our children.
Because we killed

our future.

Because we can't breathe the same air.

Because we
can't
ah ah ah
bre ah ah......... ahhe...

Words of Wisdom
inspired by Maya Angelou

Language is a tool.....
A three part triplet tool.
Born with birth scars
Intersections
Thoughts, feelings, consciousness,
Memories and expressions.

A tool as Sharp
As it is Dull.
A tool you Choose.
A tool to Use or
A tool to Abuse.
A tool to Fool
Or
To Convey, Create. Destroy. Deconstruct. Define.
A tool To Grow
Something
You never knew could.

Some say,
It's not easy.
Some say,
It's Easy **if**
You can **see** it.
Easy **if**
You can **feel** it.
Easy **if**

You can touch taste, smell, hear, know it.
Like the baby hairs
You **can't see** on
The satin side of your skin.

This second tool
The second triplet.
Doesn't look like her sister.
You **"all"** know her.
Everybody knows her name.
They call her **Change.**
Change.
Dressed in Colors
Chaos and Charms.
They call her
Change.
She says, "my tool always works."

It **works** when you
Act a new way of thinking.

When you
Think a new way of acting.

Change forever hums in your ear.
Stars in your dreams.
She is just a shadow away.

The last tool was born first.
Three Tall Triplets Tools.

Language. Change. Teach.

She is named Teach.
Teach is
the hardheaded
Trippin triplet.
She always gets **into** your head.

She'd say
I heard Maya say…
"If you **teach**, you have to <u>live</u> your teaching."
"If you **teach**, you have to <u>live</u> your teaching."

Am I doing my **best** to **live** what I teach?
Am I doing my **best** to **be** what I teach?

My grandmother use to say
When asked which tool to use
when
Times were hard
Those Times were **always** hard.

She said,
"Your Intuition is key.
Insight revealed.
Visions Colors Clear."

Lyrics spell your name
Sing them out loud.
See simple signs sideways.

Write your name
hidden inside the lines,
Underneath and above the stars.
Listen for clues,

Watch with your eyes closed.
Jump off the cliff
Open your eyes
And look up.

DayDreams are Real.
Just Like the Velveteen Rabbit."

"Just do Right. Baby."
"You know what that is."
Just do Right.

She is your Inner Twin.
She knows you more than you know her.

Mama would say,
"Try to **be** the best

Human being
Being Human
You can be."

"You **know** what **is** right."

Trust your Wisdom.

Trust your Voice.
Trust **your** Choice.

Do it.
Because **it**
IS
The only
Right thing
To do.

Being Human.

118 Days

i pledge allegiance
to the flag
of the united states of america
and to the republic
for which it stands
one nation
under God
indivisible
with liberty
and justice
for all.

Why do I know this? Why do you know this?
Why do I know Every word
Without ... Thinking?
Without ... Thinking about it?

Did we deconstruct and unpack
These concepts in our laboratories of learning
As young lambs?
Or somewhere on the streets
Of silent segregated suburbs?

Is the ease and flow
Of these wise words
As effortless
As its meanings and understandings?

Do we walk the talk?
Do we talk the walk?

Has the United States of America
Pledged Its Ideology of Unity,

Justice.
Allegiance.
Freedom.
Liberty.
To you?? To me??

The People of the United States of America
Have always stood for
And died for Freedom.
Freedom that reflects the policies,
The Will and Intentions
of All the People.
We can amend, write, march, vote
For policies written by and for the People.
For the masses.
For the millions and millions of
Unapologetic Individuals.
Old and Young.
My Children. Your Children.
Rich Children. Poor Children.

Each is different as
Loud and Silent
And those not heard.

Each is different as
Day and Night
And Those at Twilight.

Each is different as
You and Me.
And Those Unseen.

Each is different as
Those who reside in the margins
Of our democracy
Transformed and Baptized by Oppression.

Dr. Martin Luther King, Jr. said
"Will this nation rise up and live
Out the true meaning of its creed?
If America Is to Be a Great Nation
This Must BeCome True."

We must Be Come.
Become Fearless not Friendless.
Become Faithful not Hateful.
Become Hopeful not Shameful

Decolonize our Children.
Do this for our Children.
Her Children. His Children.
Their Children. Our Children.

Judge Them All
By the Content of their Character
Not by the Color of their Skin.

I remember May 2, 1963.
The clocks Stopped and Started
That early Spring Dawn.
The Plan. The Time. The Place
Was Water – Tight.
Not a detail dripped dropped out.

The Forgotten. The Untouchables.
The Black Birmingham Boys and Girls
Thousands of Them
Armed with Lunch Bags, Toothbrushes,
And Black Skin Intelligentsia.

Jumped out School Windows

Walked out Classroom
Doors Marched down
Militarized Streets For What?

For Civil Rights.
For Voting Rights.
For Human Rights.
For the Right to Live.
For the Right to Sit at the Table.

Sit at the table of Unity,
Freedom, Liberty, and Justice for All.

The Civil Rights' Soundtrack was
Singing Freedom Songs.
Black Radio stations shouted.
They jammed the airwaves.
DJs played Spirituals, Soul,
Motown's Rhythm and Blues.
The Soul of the Movement's Melody was born.

Dr. King's words were Fire.
*"Injustice Anywhere is a
Threat to Justice Everywhere."*

The Children's March
Conceived in Winter Born in Spring
Sparked 118 days of the
"Greatest Demonstration for Freedom
in the History of the Nation."
August 28, 1963.
The March for Jobs and Freedom
Washington, D.C.

Dr. King said,
*"Now is the time
To lift our national policy from the
Quicksand of Racial Injustice to
The Solid Rock of Human Dignity."*

The Dream Becomes the Promise.

*"If we protest courageously...
When the history books are written in the future,*

Somebody will have to say
'There lived a race of people...
Who had the courage to stand up for their Rights.

Their Words & Sermons
Their Spirituals & Speeches
Their Blues
Their Protest Songs
All "Found beauty in Broken Fragments of Music."

Such *"simple expressions*
Of Faith and Hope and Idealism."
This music embodied Black Youth.

"In the South, Evil stalks you
From the cradle to the grave."

Through this music. This Black Music.
"They dipped down Into the Wells of
Deeply pessimistic situations,
Danger-fraught circumstances.
To bring forth a Marvelous
Sparkling
Fluid Optimism."

They knew their *"world was dark*
And somehow, they found a ray of light."
This Light.
This Music.
Saved America.

15 Days in January

Living Daymares.
Living Nightmares.
Day and Night.

Waking Sleep.
Semi-Consciousness.
Half Alive
Half Dead.
Half Gone.
Half Left.

You Find Yourself
Juggling with Hands
Jealous of Touch.

Chasing PTSD.
Symptomatic Stains
Skin Forever.

Days Later...
Double Down
Doubled Dares
Dipped
In Eight Ounces
Of Old Fashioned
Old Time Oppression.

Seasoned with
Jim Crow's Secret Sauce.

Topped off with
Two Toxic Tablespoons of PTSS
Post Traumatic Slave Syndrome.
Dr. Joy Degruy Leary's
Personal Public Recipe.

Time...
Ticks.
Tocks.
Ticks.
Tocks.
Away.

Waiting.
Drowning.
Drowning in Oxygen
Drizzled with Deadly
Diseased Droplets.
Medical Mystery Monster
Covid -19.

Pandemic Pushed
Sensationalized
Irrational Fears
Used social media

To
Mutiny on
Washington DC.

To
Mutiny on
Washington DC.

Carloads of
Cartoon Patriots
Pulled Off
The Red.
White.
And Blue
Molded.

Festering BAND-AID

Leaving
Naked & Putrid

Exposed & Collective
Scars of Truth.
For The World to Smell.

Inside
You hear
Intestines
Moan
Intimated

Intimate
Intersectional
Irony.

Broken Promises.
Postponements.
Cancelations.
Mistrusts.
Mistakes.
Murders...

Four Minutes & Four Hundred Years Ago.

Silent Alarms
Calling All
Confused Converts
To
IMPLODE
EXPLODE
On CNN.

Mutiny on
Washington DC

Ripped Off
Lenses of Lies.

Leaving...
Calloused
Cataract
Conventions.

Leaving...
Bloodied
New Visions
Some
Still
Refuse
To See.

Remember?

One Hundred Years Ago?
One Hundred Hours Ago?
One Hundred Minutes Ago?

Mutiny on
Washington DC

Shadows Reeking of
Lynching & Sunday Picnics.

Remember?

One Hundred Years Ago?
One Hundred Hours Ago?
One Hundred Minutes Ago?

Our Ancestor's
Daymares & Nightmares?

Silently Soothed
By Loving Living Lullabies.
They Sang.
Keeping
Fires Burning.

They Sang.
Secret Coded
Songs
In the Sunlight
Of New Beginnings.

They Sang.
Songs.
Songs of Survival.
Songs of Rebirth.

Songs.
To Recollect.
To Refresh.
To Reinvent.
To Rejoice.

To
Never
Ever
Forget
Who We Are.
What We Are.
Where We Are.
When We Are.

Why We Are.
Past Tense.
Present Tense.
Future Tense.

2 Lone Winds

2 Lone Winds
Walking at midnight
Lost. Alone. Unafraid.
Lingering in the moonlight
2 Lone Winds
Following Footsteps
2 Lone Winds
Dancing with Shadowed Whispers
2 Lone Winds
Finding their way inside my dream
Leaving traces of memory
Pieces from yesterday & tomorrow.
2 Lone Winds
Ancient. Wise. Timeless.
2 Lone Winds
Coming from the East
2 Winds
I remember your
Gentle calm touch
I've seen your graceful tears
Your gifts scattered
Bits & pieces of memory
Bits & pieces from yesterday
Pieces forgotten, broken, never found
2 Lone Winds
Bringing some secret silence
2 Lone Winds decoding some mystery
Who are you? Who are you?

2020

Some Say, **2020**
Was the G.O.A.T.
Of All Years.

Some Say, **2020**
We Would Never
Forfend Forgetting.

Some Say, **2020**
We Lost
More To
Unnatural Causes,
Verses Natural Causes.

Ms. Breonna Taylor.

Mr. George Floyd.

And...
Calculatedly
Countless
More.

We Marched.
From Healdsburg
To Hong Kong.

We Sang.
Simultaneously.

BLACK LIVES MATTER.
BLACK LIVES MATTER.

We Heard.
Our Warming World
Whispering Words...

Fierce.
Fiery.
Forgotten.

Melancholy Meanings
Melting Faster
Than Arctic Ice.

Some Say, **2020**
We
Awakened.
To Truth.
To Ancient Futures.
To Ten Thousand Tomorrows.

Each Morrow
Singing...
We're Here.
We're Here.

Some Say, **2020**
Healdsburg Jazz
Took A Leap of Faith.
A Musical Metamorphosis.
A New Vision.
A New Blues Print.
Wet with the Ink of Hometown Innovation & Imagination.
Inclusive.
Diverse.
Ethnic.
Classic
Community Arts.

Close Your Eyes.
See Performers on the World Stage.
Hear Trios & Quartets
Echoing From the
Dimly Lit Courtyard of the
Healdsburg Hotel.

Snapping Fingers
Send Coded Rhythms
To Poets

Spoken Words
To Find Their Way Home
To Langston's Hideout.

Taste Wonderful Wines.
World Class.

Home Grown.
As Laughter Smiles Across Your Face.

Listen.
Watch the Artist in Residence
Reign Knowledge.
Rain Jazz Rifts.
To the Next
Generation
Of
G.O.A.T.S.

Some Say, **2020**
Fires
Burned "Us Out"
The Numbed New Normal.
No. No. No.
We Are Not NUMB.
We Are STRONG.
We Are Sonoma Strong.

We Are Black Panther Strong.
We Are **Kamala** Strong.

Flying Fearlessly on Fire to Freedom.

Some Say, **2020**
We Made "Good Trouble" Again.
We Grieved Too Many Again.

Some Say, **2020**
We Saturated
With Screens.

ZOOM.
ZOOM
DOOMED.

Facial
Accessories
Fashionable.
Kanye.
AKA Yeezy
Ran for POTUS?

Some Say, **2020**
Historical.
Hysterical.
Hurtful.
Hopeful.
Yes.
Hopeful.
Some Say, **2020**
Intuitive.
Inspirational.
Introspective & Intimate
Intersection of
All Time & Space.

Some Say, **2020**
Millions & Millions
Of Musical
Muse Messengers
Sheltered in Place
With Us.

Hidden.
Helplessly in Plain Sight.
Saying...

WE ARE HERE.

WE ARE ALIVE.

WE ARE NOW.

WE...
ARE.

93% Stardust

We have
Cherished Chattel Calcium in our Bones.
Blessed with Mother Land Chocolate Milk.
We have
Innate infinite iron in our Veins.
Red. Black. Green.

We have
Indigo Blood Cells Burnt Bittersweet.
Living History DNA Glimpses,
Fever Flashbacks & Visions.
Traces of Transient Traumatized
Black Farmers' Secret Scars
Stained with
Crystal Cut Copper
Carefully Carved from
Stolen Sticks & Stones.

We have
Catastrophic Carbon in our Souls.
Ebony Constellations.
Drops of Blackened Ash.
Smoked Kissed by
Jim Crow's Charred Chapped Lips
Whispering micro aggressions
that Never Stopped Our Flow.

We have
Navigating Nitrogen in our Brains.
Chemical reactions trigger Elegant Sweat,
Thanksgiving Tears,
 Sweet Dreams & Sweet Realities.
Remember Revolution
Remembers Everything.

We are
93% Stardust.
Celestial Covert Raindrops.
Morning Moonbeams wet with dew.
Cosmic "Colored Only" Memories
Cake walks downtown 4th Street
Throwing Shade Sipping Tea.

We are
Left-handed Shadows
On Southside Sidewalks
Listening to Hearts humming hymns.
Sliding out sunlit windows on Sunday mornings.

We are
Homespun Struggles and Traumas.
Homemade Histories. Lost & Found Legacies.
Broken Promises. Postponed Afro-Futures.
Darken Destiny Dust Dissipate Daughters' Dreams.

We are
Siren Spiritual Souls

Baptized in fiery iced Onyx.
Praying
Remember - Remember Who We Are.

We are
Standing in Sankofa's Shoes.
Believers of Black Girl Magic Nursery Rhymes.
Melanin Metamorphic Mastodontic Moments
Becoming Blue Black Blood Diamonds
That Never Ever Die.
We are.
We are 93%
StarDust.

95
A poem for Areatha

95.
95 Reasons to Love You.
95 Dancing Dreams
Waiting to Come True.
95 Whispering Wishes
Waiting for You.
95 Kisses and Hugs too.

95 Words seem so small
Compared to the
Millions And Millions of Wise Words
You Have Given to Us All.

95 Powerful
Passionate Prayers
All Have been Answered.
With Many More to Spare.

Because
We Know for Sure
God Sends His Love
To Your Door.

95 Dainty Daydreams Designed
To Make You Smile.

95 Splendid spoonful's
Of Areatha's Soulful Cooking Styles.

95 Minutes on the phone,
Goes too fast.
95 More Moments to make it last.
95 Sweet Spiritual Hymns
Shout and Sing.

95 Bells Ring and Ring.
"A r e a t h a"
"A r e a t h a"

95 Voices Harmonize
Your Love.
Your Kindness.
Your Creative Caring.

95 Pretty Presents.
95 Poems
All Over the Place.
95 Smiles
All Over My Face.

95 Valentines sent each year.
95 Giggles to tickle your ears.
95 Miles to Race to Your Door.
95 Hours of Laughter and Joy.

95 Stories to share.
95 Examples of your
AMAZING GRACE.

95 Ways to say...
Happy Birthday AREATHA.

**WE LOVE YOU
MORE AND
MORE AND
MORE...**

98
A tribute poem in honor of Areatha Sims

98.
98 Reasons to Love You.
98 Dancing Dreams
98 Whispering Wishes
Waiting for You.
98 Kisses & 98 Hugs.

98 Words seem so small.
Compared to the
Millions & Millions & Millions
Of Wise Wonderful Words
You have given Us all.

98 Powerful Passionate Prayers
All Answered.
With Many More to Spare.
Because.
We know for sure.
God Is never late.
Sending His Love
To **Your** Door.

98 Dainty Delicate
Daydreams Designed
To Make You Smile.

98 Splendid Sweet & Savory
Mouth Watering Spoonful's
Of Areatha's Soulful
"You Put Your Foot In it"
Cooking Styles.

98 Minutes talking on the phone.
Goes too fast.
98 More Moments to make it last.

98 Sweet Spiritual Hymns
Shout and Sing.
98 Bells Ring & Ring & Ring.
A r e a t h a.

98 Voices Sing in Pitch Perfect Harmony.
98 Praises of Your Loyal Lasting Love.
Your Kind Spirit.
Your Creative Caring.
Your Sense of Humor.
Your Unconditional Non-Judgement.

98 Perfect Days to Pray & Pray.
98 Poems
98 Pretty Presents
All over the place.
98 Smiles
All over **your** face.

98 Valentines sent every year.
98 Giggles to tickle your ears.
98 Miles to Race to your door.
98 Hours of Laughter and Joy.

98 Sacred Stories you shared.
98 Memories to last a lifetime.
98 Lessons, you taught us each day.
98 Stars write out your name at night.

98 Praises of your
Amazing Grace.
98 Cheers & Songs of Devotion.
98 Ways to show our Respect & Forever Gratitude.

98 Angels waiting to welcome **you** home.
98 Blessings hiding in your pocket.
98 Candles on your heavenly cake.

98 Jewels placed in your heavenly crown.
98 Ways to say.
We love **you,** Areatha.
Always & in All Ways.
We Love You
More & More & More & More.

About the Author

Enid Pickett is a poet, writer, and teacher. With over 30 years of teaching experience, she has served as a master teacher at Sonoma State University, as well as on the Advisory Board of Learning for Justice. She also trained with NEA Human and Civil Rights Department as a Diversity Trainer for 15 years, and she was a Commissioner on the Status of Women in Sonoma County.

Enid sang in the Healdsburg Freedom Jazz Choir for several years. In 2020, she became the Poet Laureate for Healdsburg Jazz. She has appeared at the San Francisco Jazz Center and The Raven Theater. She is one of the founding members of an Edutainment Women's Collective, The Nubian Café Collective. Enid lives in Sonoma County Wine Country, Windsor, California.

enidpickett.com

www.ingramcontent.com/pod-product-compliance
Lightning Source LLC
Chambersburg PA
CBHW071702120626
46550CB00001B/75